The Art of the Handmade Quilt

Nancy Brenan Daniel

STERLING

New York / London
www.sterlingpublishing.com

Produced by

Production Team

Creative Directors: Rita Weiss
                                  Jean Leinhauser

Editorial Director: Linda Causee

Photography: Carol Wilson Mansfield

Technical Editors: Ann Harnden
                                  Christina Wilson

Book Design: Linda Causee

Acknowledgements

Special thanks to Rita Weiss and Linda Causee. Although my name appears on the cover as author of this book, no part of it was accomplished alone. I am indebted to these editors who have given me good advice during my work and who have paid close attention to the details of producing the book as you see it. They have always been a source of generous advice and encouragement.

This book acknowledges the many quilters who inspire me by their quilts, in my research, and in my classrooms. I am forever in their debt.

Some of the anonymous quilters are represented by quilts illustrated in this book. Although we don't know their names, their needlework tells us much about them. I am grateful to these wonderful, though nameless, quilters. They are my pathfinders. Like contemporary quiltmakers they show us thrift, resourcefulness, creativity, and individuality.

A quiltmaker, and an author, can never have too much encouragement from family, friends, teachers, and other fellow professionals. Knowing I will forget far too many, I nevertheless, want to also thank the following people for exhibiting special support by their actions, words and work through my professional life: Meredith Montross; Bobbie Matela; Karey Bresenhan; Judy Murrah; Anita Murphy; Ann Armstrong; Yvonne Porcella; Jean Ray Laury; Anne Dutton; Dorothy Dodds; elinor peace bailey; Ruth Dahn; Louise Waltermeyer; Marjorie Fetterhoff; Meredith Schroeder; Sandra Hatch; Jane Hall; Dixie Haywood...

Thank you Grandma Ritzenthaler for teaching me to love everything about quilts—and thank you Mom for teaching me to love.

Nancy Brenan Daniel

STERLING and the distinctive Sterling logo are registered trademarks of Sterling Publishing Co., Inc.

Library of Congress Cataloging-in-Publication Data Available

10 9 8 7 6 5 4 3 2 1

Published by Sterling Publishing Co., Inc.
387 Park Avenue South, New York, NY 10016
© 2008 by The Creative Partners™ LLC
Distributed in Canada by Sterling Publishing
c/o Canadian Manda Group, 165 Dufferin Street,
Toronto, Ontario, Canada M6K 3H6
Distributed in the United Kingdom by GMC Distribution Services,
Castle Place, 166 High Street, Lewes, East Sussex, England BN7 1XU
Distributed in Australia by Capricorn Link (Australia) Pty. Ltd.
P.O. Box 704, Windsor, NSW 2756, Australia

Printed in China

Sterling ISBN-13: 978-1-4027-3351-2
           ISBN-10: 1-4027-3351-8

For information about custom editions, special sales, premium and corporate purchases, please contact Sterling Special Sales Department at 800-805-5489 or specialsales@sterlingpublishing.com.

Introduction

Textiles, bedding in particular, are a part of human history. They are a tangible record of the things of everyday living and the socio-economic history of nations young and old. To study textiles, one must look into the social and economic development of civilizations as well as the state of technology at any one time in history. It makes for very interesting study. A quilt can tell us a lot about the maker and about the conditions that prompted the maker to take needle to cloth and create the quilt.

Quiltmaking today is a fascinating hobby. The study and collection of quilts can also offer pleasure to those who want to learn more about the quilt and the life and times of its creator. I hope that this book will satisfy both the collector of quilts and quiltmakers whether their interest is casual or avid.

Have you longed to make a quilt but can't fathom how you would begin? Quilts of patchwork or appliqué are possible for even a beginner. A modest investment in basic tools and supplies and some experience with specific stitches and techniques will start one on a lifetime of pleasure. Learning to make a quilt will also help one to appreciate the quilts she owns, collects, or inherits.

In the twenty-first century we take a special satisfaction in owning and creating both artful and utilitarian quilts for ourselves and our homes. Quilts made by hand are as treasured today as are the quilts made before the advent of the sewing machine in the nineteenth century.

Why, when even the most common needle-sewn thing can be made quicker and cheaper at home or in factories by machine—why make anything by hand?

There is a special joy and sense of fulfillment that accompanies the time spent doing needlework by hand. I think it's the directness of the labor. There are only simple devises between the maker and the work—needle, thread and bits of cloth are all that are really needed. Handwork endures because it can be done in small pockets of time and in almost any location. People can be seen pulling out their patchwork or appliqué in the most unusual locations - airports, busses, doctors' offices, sporting and entertainment events and lectures.

The current revival of quiltmaking began in the last quarter of the twentieth century when many revisited the craft in anticipation of the American Bicentennial. Most States began extensive quilt searches to establish and locate the history, travel, and economic circumstances of American culture by the examination of family quilts. Quilts can tell fascinating stories and raise interesting questions even if the maker is unknown. Think about it. What kind of fabric…wool, cotton, silk? Was it from an old dress or man's shirt or new? What was the skill level needed—what tools were to be had? Was it made by a man or woman - or a group? Each quilt has a story and its own beauty.

Some of my Grandmother's quilts contain scraps of fabrics I gave her left over from sundresses and sun-suits I made for my children. Each time I trail my hands over her handmade quilts I touch each fabric as a tangible link and memory of her as she joyfully pieced her quilts—sitting in the glider under the front porch light on many a summer evening.

Beyond the technical aspects of making a quilt there is the reverence for the history and tradition of the quilt. It is a love of handwork as a connection to our past and those we love. More importantly, it is the need for quiet, productive activity in our lives. Many people who enjoy hand work in quiltmaking liken it to a form of meditation. Does that mean those machine-made quilts are second rate—not at all! Even after you have learned the techniques for making a quilt by hand, you may choose to do some machine work on your quilt—feel free to do it, especially on the seams over 18" or longer. Quilters have used the sewing machine since the first hand-cranked machine was patented in 1846—two years before gold was discovered in California.

Contents

Birds in the Air Stars

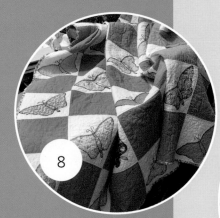

Butterflies

Prickly Pear Medallion

Honey Bee Sampler

Red Nine-Patch

Flowers of Friendship

Star Studded

Comet Catcher

Indiana Puzzle

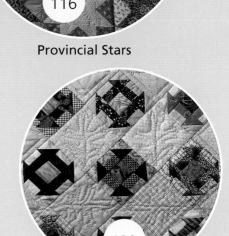

Provincial Stars

Windblown Daisy

Shoo-fly

Appliqué Medallion

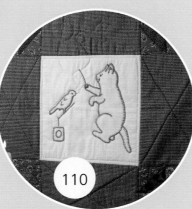

Whig Rose

Summertime

The Music Lesson

Courthouse Steps Log Cabin

Evening Star

Let's Begin....

There are many possibilities in quiltmaking and there are many decisions to consider in order for the quiltmaking to go forward with the most pleasure for you and the least amount of frustration. Everyone will become discouraged from time to time during the process. You will want to hurry up the process. You might decide a choice of fabric or technique was possibly the wrong one and you might be tempted to quit—mid-quilt.

Those are very natural feelings when learning something new. Even experienced quilters often have doubts about their choices and their skills. Just relax and enjoy each step of the process. Making a quilt is like running a marathon. Consider each step forward as moving toward your goal and remember, most of the pleasure in quiltmaking is the journey. Along the way you will learn some new skills and gain added respect for the family quilts you may have admired for years.

Read through the following technique sections of the book. Practice the techniques perhaps by making a small project before you begin one of the larger quilts.

Where to Begin…

The needle skills that you already have before beginning to quilt will facilitate learning the new language and skills of quilt making. If making a quilt will be your first needlework project please take note of the skill rating given to each quilt and let that be your guide. The ratings range from one needle (beginner) to four needles (expert).

The rating only indicates the level or needle skills the average quilter will need to be successful with the project. The rating does not indicate how much time a project will take.

Butterflies

Approximate Size

72" x 80"

Block Size

8" x 8" finished

Materials

Blocks
3 yards pink (alternate squares)
3 yards white or muslin (background)
45 scraps assorted print and solids (8" x 8" each)
Template material
4 skeins black embroidery floss
Embroidery needle
Erasable fabric marker

Finishing
Full/queen-size batting (76" x 84")
5 yards backing

Pattern

Butterfly Appliqué Pattern (page 12)
Flower Quilting Design (page 12)
Alternate Block Quilting Design (page 13)

Note: *See General Directions, page 146, for making and using templates – remember the seam allowance. Make two templates for the Butterfly—one template for the wings and one for the body.*

Cutting

45 squares each, 8½" x 8½", pink and white
45 Butterfly Wings, assorted prints and solids

This quilt was rescued from an estate sale. The seller knew nothing about this lovely old quilt from the 1930s. It must have meant something to the original owner because it has never been used and is in excellent condition. The appliquéd Butterflies are most likely from a mail-order source. There are no repeat fabrics used in any of the Butterflies – even though some of the solid colors are similar they are not the same – there are slight differences. Perhaps the maker combined two kits – one of solid and one of print butterflies. The backing is in a bold print. The quilting design is a typical papercut style favored in that period – these were cut like paper snowflakes. It's a shame we don't know more about the quilt or quiltmaker. This quilt is a reminder for quiltmakers to label their quilts!

Instructions

Note: *Please read Appliqué Quilts, pages 147 to 155, before beginning.*

Making the Blocks

1. Fold an 8½" x 8½" white square in quarters. Pin or baste the prepared appliqué to the background fabric. (**Diagram 1**)

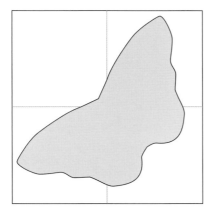

Diagram 1

2. Stitch the Butterfly to the background fabric with small even stitches. Repeat for all 45 Butterfly blocks.

3. Separate an 18" to 22" piece of floss into two or three strands. Thread an embroidery needle and sew the Blanket Stitch around the edge of the Butterfly. (**Diagram 2**) Repeat for all 45 Butterfly Blocks.

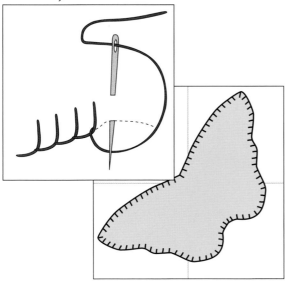

Diagram 2

4. Place the Butterfly body template over a Butterfly. Trace around the template lightly with an erasable fabric marker. This is your embroidery line. (**Diagram 3**)

Diagram 3

5. Embroider the body with three strands of black embroidery floss using the Stem Stitch. (**Diagram 4**) Take small stitches. Repeat for all 45 Butterfly Blocks.

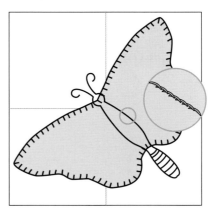

Diagram 4

Finishing

Note: *Read Finishing Up, pages 161 to 174, to complete your quilt.*

1. Lay out ten rows of blocks alternating 8½" x 8½" pink squares and Butterfly blocks. (**Diagram 5**)

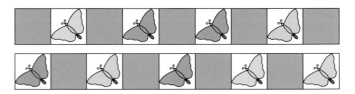

Diagram 5

2. Join the individual blocks in rows and then join the rows together. This can be done by hand or machine.

3. Mark the Alternate Block Quilting Design in the pink blocks using an erasable fabric marker. (**Diagram 6**)

Diagram 6

4. Mark the Flower Quilting Design in the Butterfly blocks using an erasable fabric marker. (**Diagram 7**)

Diagram 7

5. Piece and cut backing so it extends about 2" beyond each edge.

6. Layer the quilt top, batting and backing together with the wrong sides of the quilt top and backing facing the batting. Baste or pin the layers together. Hand quilt the motifs in each block.

7. Finish the edge of the quilt by turning the backing fabric toward the front. Fold the raw edge under and hand stitch down along folded edge.

8. Add a label on the quilt back.

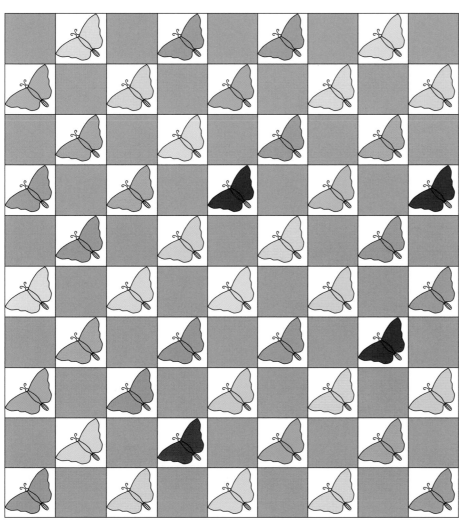

Butterfly Quilt Layout

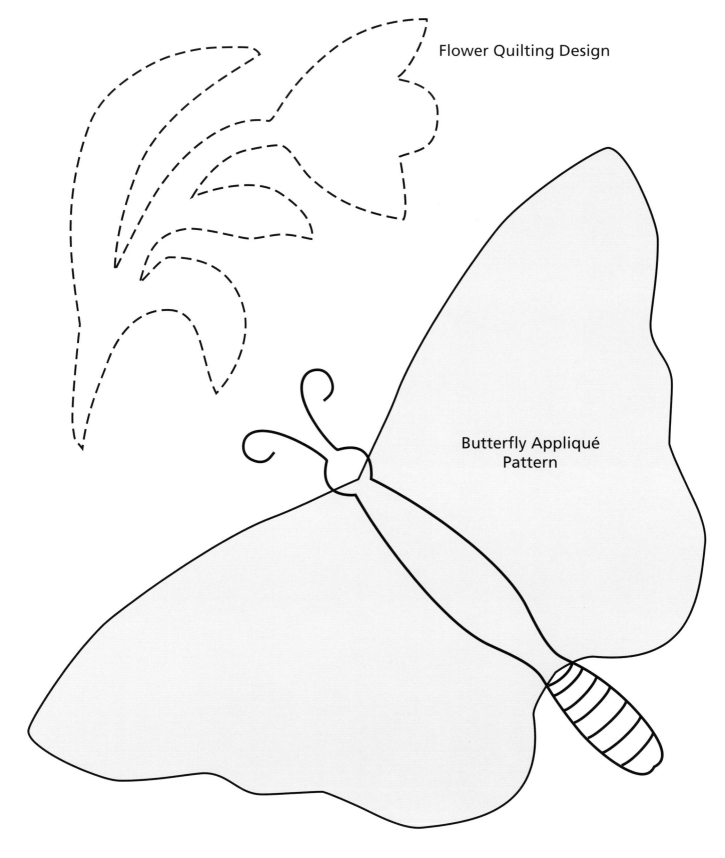

Flower Quilting Design

Butterfly Appliqué
Pattern

Alternate Block Quilting Design

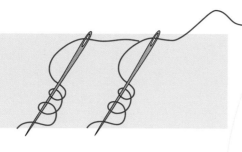

Honey Bee Sampler

Approximate Size
43" x 43"

Honey Bee Block Size
15" x 15" finished

Small Block Size
5" x 5" finished

Notes: *Please read the General Directions, pages 142 to 174, before you begin. Fabric quantities specified are for 42" - 44" wide, 100% cotton fabrics. Templates* **do not** *include seam allowances. Strip-cut measurements* **do** *include seam allowances. Use a ¼" seam allowance. Sew with right sides together. Press seams as you go.*

Materials

Blocks
¼ yard black
¼ yard gold
¼ yard black print (there are two prints in the sample quilt)
¼ yard or scraps of several coordinating scrap prints (gold, rust, gold/black)
⅔ yard light background (pieced blocks and setting squares)
⅓ yard medium background (setting and corner triangles)

Finishing
⅜ yard blue
1⅛ yards floral print
48" x 48" batting and backing

Patterns

Honey Bee (page 22)
Strips and Squares (page 23)
Double X (page 23)
Cake Stand (page 23)
Kaleidoscope Patch (page 23)
Ohio Star (page 23)
Flower Basket (page 24)
Duck and Ducklings (page 24)
Dutchman's Puzzle (page 24)
Eight-pointed Star (page 24)
Setting Triangle, Corner Triangle and Setting Square (page 25)

There are twelve small blocks and one large Honey Bee block in this sampler. The Honey Bee Block is an excellent size and a perfect block design for the beginning hand sewer. You will learn about piecing, appliqué, sashing and borders in this one central block. The setting for the sampler and the additional small blocks are designed to hold your interest in completing the quilt. Don't be afraid of their small size. Each block can be stitched by hand during two or three evening television shows.

As you work you will be intrigued by the names of the quilt blocks. Some names are obvious – like "Dutchman's Puzzle". One can see the whirls of a windmill. Others are not so obvious – compare the "Ohio Star" block with the "True Eight-pointed Star." Both have eight points to the star…so…why…? TRADITION. Many blocks have several different names depending on the place the block was made or at what time in history the block or quilt was made or when that block or design was 'captured' by a quilt historian and preserved for our use today. One quilter will call a block "Monkey Wrench" – and another quilter will call the same block "Puss in the Corner" – and both quilters will be correct. Fascinating! When you design your own quilt or special block…you may name it anything you please.

Cutting

Note: *Each block in the sampler has its own set of templates. They may look the same, but create and label each template for each block. Place each set of templates in a separate, labeled, plastic baggie.*

Center Block: Honey Bee
Note: *Make plastic templates for A, B, C, D, and E. Label the templates with all notations.*

4 A Squares, black
4 B Rectangles, gold
1 C Square, black print
4 D Honey Bee Bodies, gold
8 E Honey Bee Wings, gold/black print scrap
2 rectangles, $3\frac{1}{2}$" x $9\frac{1}{2}$", light background
2 rectangles, $3\frac{1}{2}$" x $15\frac{1}{2}$", light background

Sampler Block 1: Strips and Squares
Note: *Make plastic templates for A, B and C. Label the templates with all notations.*

16 A Squares, black
16 B Rectangles, gold
4 C Squares, black print

Sampler Block 2: Double X
Note: *Make plastic templates for A and B. Label the templates with all notations.*

6 A Triangles, light background
6 A Triangles, blue print scraps
2 B Squares, light background
1 B Square, black print

Sampler Block 3: Cake Stand
Note: *Make plastic templates for A, B, C and D. Label the templates with all notations.*

1 A Square, light background
4 B Triangles, light background
4 B Triangles, rust print scraps
2 B Triangles, black
2 C Rectangles, light background
1 D Triangle, bright yellow scrap
1 D Triangle, black print
1 D Triangle, light background

Sampler Block 4: Kaleidoscope Patch
Note: *Make plastic templates for A and B. Label the templates with all notations.*

4 A Triangles, light background
4 B Triangles, gold
4 B Triangles, black print

Sampler Block 5: Flower Basket
Note: *Make plastic templates for A, B and C. Label the templates with all notations.*

8 A Triangles, light background
6 A Triangles, assorted scraps
2 A Triangles, dark gold scraps
2 B Rectangles, light background
1 C Triangle, light background
1 C Triangle, dark gold scraps

Sampler Block 6: Ohio Star
Note: *Make plastic templates for A and B. Label the templates with all notations.*

4 A Squares, light background
1 A Square, black print
4 B Triangles, light background
8 B Triangles, blue scraps
4 B Triangles, gold

Sampler Block 7: Duck and Ducklings
Note: *Make plastic templates for A, B, C and D. Label the templates with all notations.*

5 A Squares, gold
8 B Triangles, light background
4 C Rectangles, light background
4 D Triangles, black print

Sampler Block 8: Dutchman's Puzzle
Note: *Make plastic templates for A and B. Label the templates with all notations.*

12 A Triangles, light background
4 A Triangles, blue scraps
4 B Triangles, tan scraps
4 B Triangles, rust scraps

Sampler Block 9: Eight-pointed Star
Note: *Make plastic templates for A, B and C. Label the templates with all notations.*

4 A Squares, light background
4 B Diamonds, black print
4 B Diamonds, black
4 C Triangles, light background

Finishing Squares and Triangles
Note: *Make plastic templates for Corner Triangles, Setting Triangles and Setting Squares. Label the templates with all notations.*

4 Corner Triangles, medium background
12 Setting Triangles, medium background
4 Setting Squares, $5\frac{1}{2}$" x $5\frac{1}{2}$", light background

4 strips, 2½" x width of fabric, blue (first border)

4 squares, 2½" x 2½", black (first border corner-stones)

4 strips, 6" x width of fabric, floral print (second border)

4 strips 2½" x width of fabric, floral print (binding)

Instructions

The Honey Bee Block

1. Lay out patchwork pieces A, B, and C for Honey Bee Block. Set aside the appliqué pieces. Stitch the patches together. (**Diagram 1**)

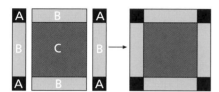

Diagram 1

2. Sew 3½" x 9½" light background rectangles to top and bottom; sew 3½" x 15½" light background rectangles to sides. (**Diagram 2**)

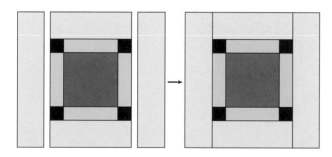

Diagram 2

3. Prepare the appliqué Bee Bodies D and Bee Wings E and stitch to the Honey Bee block referring to Appliqué Quilts, pages 147 to 155. (**Diagram 3**)

Diagram 3   Honey Bee Block

Tip: *Take a moment to look at the finished Honey Bee Block. You can see the anatomy of a quilt in this one block: there is a central square; sashing surrounds the square; there is a border embellished with appliqué.*

Strips and Squares

1. Lay out patchwork pieces A, B and C for a Strips and Squares block. Sew block referring to **Diagram 4**. Make three more blocks. Place the finished blocks in a plastic baggie until time to assemble the quilt.

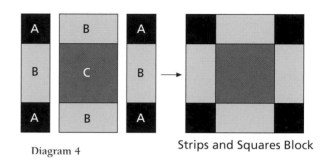

Diagram 4   Strips and Squares Block

Double X

1. Lay out patchwork pieces A and B for a Double X block. Sew block referring to **Diagram 5**. Place the finished block in a plastic baggie until time to assemble the quilt.

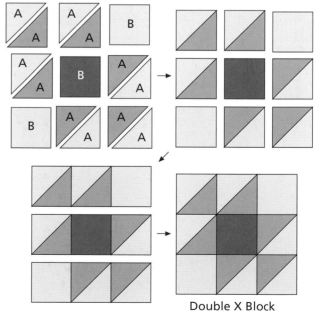

Diagram 5   Double X Block

17

Cake Stand

1. Lay out patchwork pieces A, B, C and D for a Cake Stand block. Sew block referring to **Diagram 6.** Place the finished block in a plastic baggie until time to assemble the quilt.

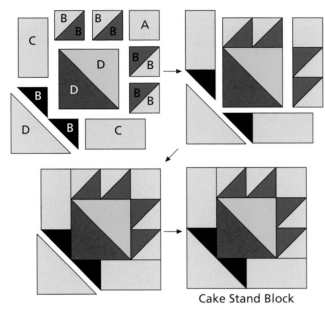

Cake Stand Block

Diagram 6

Flower Basket

1. Lay out patchwork pieces A, B and C for a Flower Basket block. Sew block referring to **Diagram 8**. Place the finished block in a plastic baggie until time to assemble the quilt.

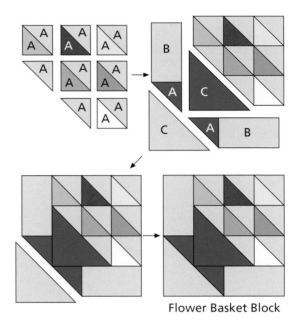

Flower Basket Block

Diagram 8

Kaleidoscope Patch

1. Lay out patchwork pieces A and B for a Kaleidoscope block. Sew block referring to **Diagram 7**. Place the finished block in a plastic baggie until time to assemble the quilt.

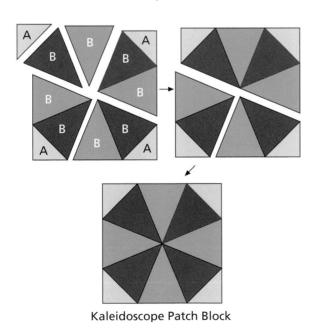

Kaleidoscope Patch Block

Diagram 7

Ohio Star

1. Lay out patchwork pieces A and B for an Ohio Star block. Sew block referring to **Diagram 9**. Place the finished block in a plastic baggie until time to assemble the quilt.

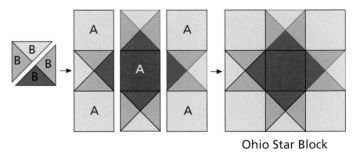

Ohio Star Block

Diagram 9

18

Duck and Ducklings

1. Lay out patchwork pieces A, B, C and D for a Duck and Ducklings block. Sew block referring to **Diagram 10**. Place the finished block in a plastic baggie until time to assemble the quilt.

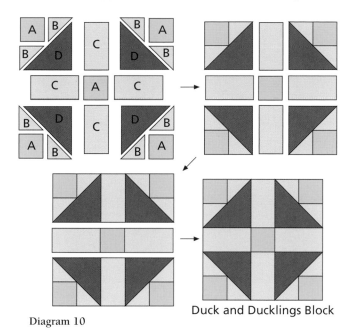

Duck and Ducklings Block

Diagram 10

Dutchman's Puzzle

1. Lay out patchwork pieces A and B for a Dutchman's Puzzle block. Sew block referring to **Diagram 11**. Place the finished block in a plastic baggie until time to assemble the quilt.

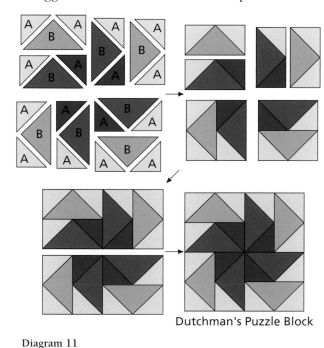

Dutchman's Puzzle Block

Diagram 11

Eight-pointed Star

1. Lay out patchwork pieces A, B and C for an Eight-pointed Star block. Sew block referring to **Diagram 12**. Place the finished block in a plastic baggie until time to assemble the quilt.

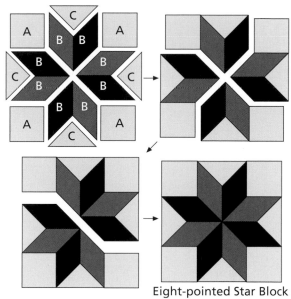

Eight-pointed Star Block

Diagram 12

Finishing the Quilt

Note: *Read Finishing Up, pages 161 to 174, to complete your quilt.*

1. Lay out the Honey Bee Block, the twelve sampler blocks, and the four Setting Squares. Pay attention to the position of the Basket block and Cake Stand block. They are directional. (**Diagram 13**)

Diagram 13

2. Next, position the Corner Triangles and Setting Triangles. (**Diagram 14**)

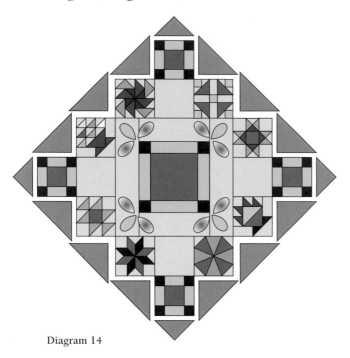

Diagram 14

3. Assemble each corner section as illustrated. (**Diagram 15**)

Diagram 15

4. Stitch each corner section to the central Honey Bee Block. (**Diagram 16**)

Diagram 16

5. For first border, measure all sides of the quilt and cut the four 2½"-wide blue strips to this measurement. Sew a strip to the top and bottom of quilt top. Sew a 2½" black square to each end of remaining 2½"-wide blue strips. Sew to sides of quilt. (**Diagram 17**)

Diagram 17

6. For second border, measure the quilt crosswise. Cut two 6"-wide black print strips to that measurement. Sew to the sides of the quilt. Measure quilt lengthwise. Cut two 6"-wide black print strips and sew to the top and bottom of the quilt.

7. Layer the quilt top, batting and backing together with the wrong sides of the quilt top and backing facing the batting. Baste or pin the layers together. Quilt as desired.

8. Finish the edge of the quilt with continuous binding. Add a label on the quilt back.

Honey Bee Sampler Quilt Layout

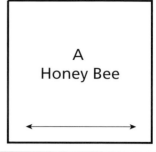

A
Honey Bee

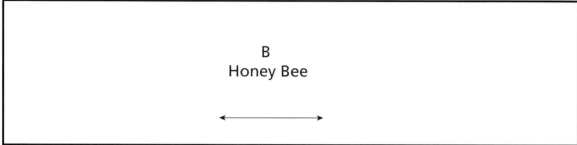

B
Honey Bee

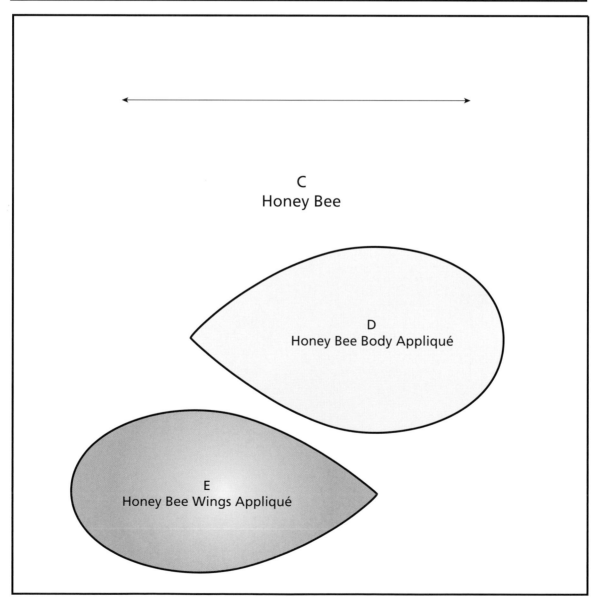

C
Honey Bee

D
Honey Bee Body Appliqué

E
Honey Bee Wings Appliqué

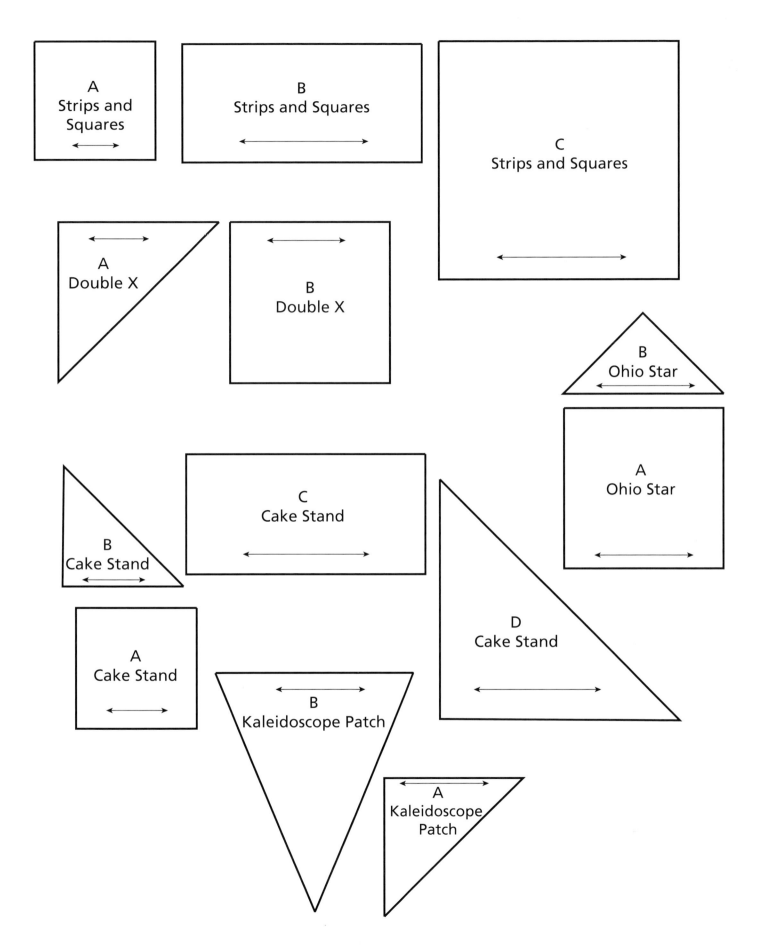

A
Strips and Squares

B
Strips and Squares

C
Strips and Squares

A
Double X

B
Double X

B
Ohio Star

A
Ohio Star

B
Cake Stand

C
Cake Stand

D
Cake Stand

A
Cake Stand

B
Kaleidoscope Patch

A
Kaleidoscope Patch

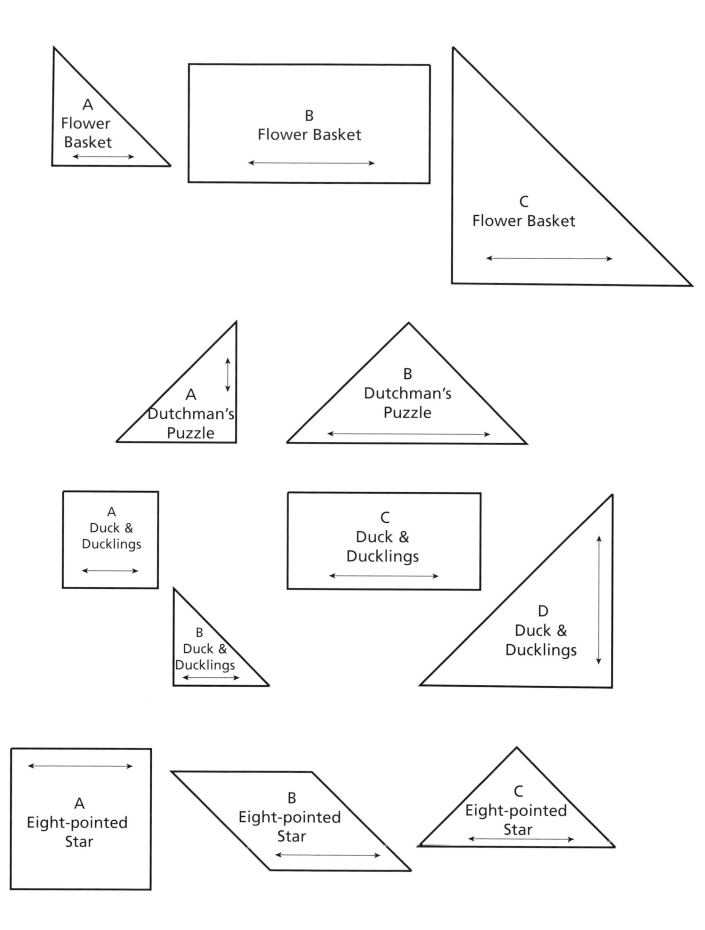

A
Flower
Basket

B
Flower Basket

C
Flower Basket

A
Dutchman's
Puzzle

B
Dutchman's
Puzzle

A
Duck &
Ducklings

C
Duck &
Ducklings

D
Duck &
Ducklings

B
Duck &
Ducklings

A
Eight-pointed
Star

B
Eight-pointed
Star

C
Eight-pointed
Star

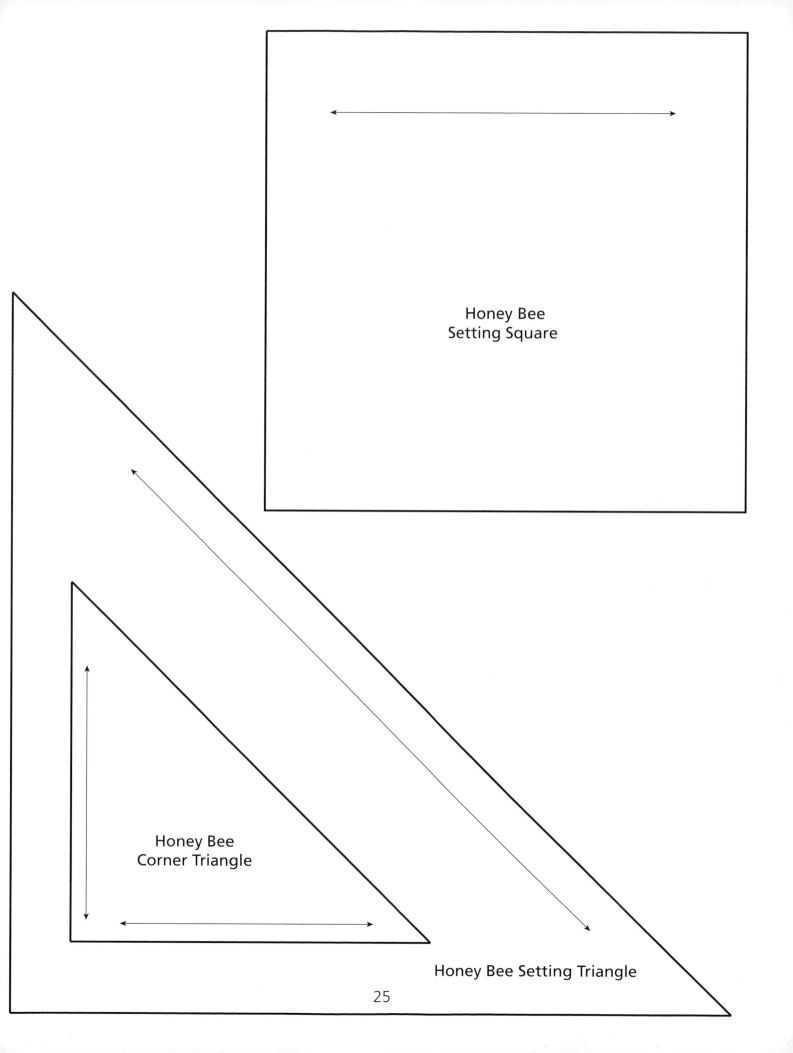

Honey Bee
Setting Square

Honey Bee
Corner Triangle

Honey Bee Setting Triangle

25

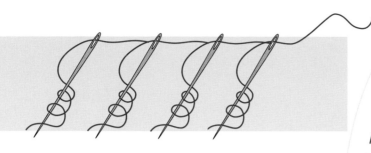

Flowers of Friendship

Approximate Size
36" x 36"

Block Size
3" x 3" finished

Notes: *Please read the General Directions, pages 142 to 174, before you begin. Fabric quantities specified are for 42" - 44" wide, 100% cotton. Templates **do not** include seam allowances. Strip cut measurements **do** include seam allowances. Sew with right sides together. Press seams as you go.*

Materials

Pieced and Appliqué Blocks
¾ yard light background print
½ yard medium background print
½ yard rose solid or small print (pieced flowers)
¼ yard dark green/brown print (pieced and appliquéd leaves)
½ yard medium green (stems, border leaves)
⅛ yard gold print (flower centers)
Erasable fabric marker
One skein black embroidery floss and embroidery needle

Finishing
½ yard medium background print (first border)
1⅛ yards border stripe print (second border)
¼ yard dark floral (binding)
40" x 40" batting and backing

Note: *Make precision templates for each of the pieced and appliquéd parts of the quilt. Take your time making these small templates. Remember to label each template and keep them safely in a plastic baggie with the cut fabric. Use a separate baggie for each template – some of the pieces are very similar in size and shape. Label each baggie.*

This quilt is a classic, centrally organized, medallion-style design. All of the design elements in the quilt relate to each other around the central focal point of flowers in the lighter background fabric. The larger, fully blossoming Carolina Lily flowers, draw the eye to the border of linked flower buds in the darker second background fabric.

The title of the quilt was chosen first for this original quilt. The buds and full flowers represent the changing patterns and growth of friendships.

One of the more interesting features is the use of both piecing and appliqué techniques in the leaves and the use of patterned fabric for the leaf shapes.

A second prominent feature is the use of blocks and border elements that combine both straight settings and settings on point to create a unified, but dynamic setting for this contemporary quilt classic.

The fabrics, colors, and attention to fine, detailed handwork mark this small quilt as remarkable and timeless.

Patterns

Templates A to O (pages 34 to 36)
Border Vine Placement (page 35)
Center Vine Placement (page 36)
Full Flower Quilting Pattern (page 37)
Partial Flower Quilting Pattern (page 37)

Cutting

Note: *For piecing the blocks and the body of the quilt, trace the templates then cut these pieces from fabric.*

Quilt Center

4 A, light background print
4 B, light background print
4 D, light background print
4 E, light background print
4 C and 4 C reversed, rose solid or small print
4 A, gold print
4 C and 4 C reversed, dark green/brown print

Flower Blocks

12 A, light background print
12 B, light background print
36 F, light background print
48 G, light background print
36 C and 36 C reversed, rose solid or small print
12 C and 12 C reversed, dark green/brown print
12 A, gold print

Triangle Flower Buds

4 A, medium background print
4 B, medium background print
8 G, medium background print
8 H, medium background print
4 C and 4 C reversed, rose solid or small print
4 C and 4 C reversed, dark green/brown print
4 A, gold print

Partial Triangle Flower Buds A and B

8 A, medium background print
8 B, medium background print
8 A, gold print
8 C and 8 C reversed, rose solid or small print
8 C and 8 C reversed, dark green/brown print
16 G, medium background print
8 H, medium background print

Appliqué

52 (or more) N, dark green/brown print
46 (or more) O, medium green
6 yards, $\frac{1}{4}$"-wide bias strips for stems (see Making Bias Strips, page 152), medium green

Finishing

4 I, light background print
4 J, light background print
8 K, light background print
8 L, light background print
4 M, medium background print

4 strips, $2\frac{1}{2}$" x width of fabric, medium background (first border)
4 strips, $3\frac{1}{2}$" x width of fabric, border stripe print (second border)
4 strips, 2" x width of fabric, dark floral (binding)

Note: *You may need to adjust the width of the second border to accommodate the size of the individual stripes in your fabric.*

Instructions

Quilt Center

Center Block

1. Sew a light background print A Square to a gold print A Square. Sew pair of Squares to a light background print B Rectangle. (**Diagram 1**) Repeat for three more units.

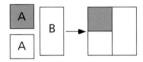

Diagram 1

2. Referring to **Diagram 2**, sew units together in pairs then sew pairs together. Set aside.

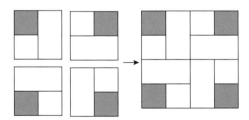

Diagram 2

3. Sew a rose C Diamond to a dark green/brown print C Diamond reversed. Make four pairs, then make four more pairs with rose C Diamonds reversed and dark green/brown print C Diamonds.

Press the pieced Diamond seams open as you go. (**Diagram 3**)

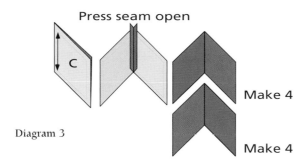

Press seam open

C

Make 4

Make 4

Diagram 3

Note: *Review the technique for Sewing Inset Seams, page 161.*

4. Sew a light background print D Square between pairs of Diamonds made in step 3 to complete the diagonal units. (**Diagram 4**)

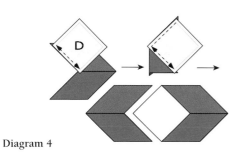

D

Diagram 4

5. Sew a light background E Triangle to the dark green/brown print side of each diagonal unit to form corner units. (**Diagram 5**)

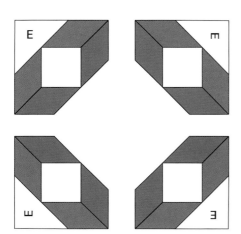

E

E

E

E

Diagram 5

6. Sew the corner units to opposite sides of the center unit made in step 2. (**Diagram 6**)

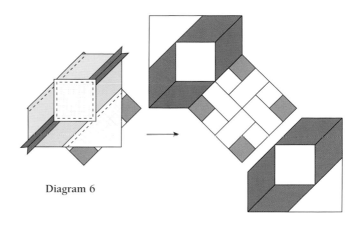

Diagram 6

7. Sew the last two sides to the middle. (**Diagram 7**)

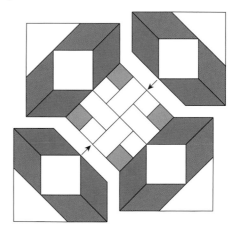

Diagram 7

8. Sew the connecting seams from the middle toward the edge of the center. (**Diagram 8**)

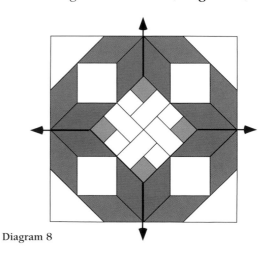

Diagram 8

9. Sew the light background I pieces to each side of center. Sew joining seams from inside to outside edge. (**Diagram 9**)

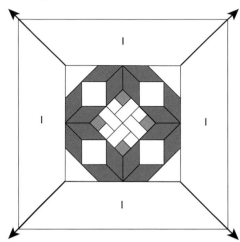

Diagram 9

Flower Blocks

1. Sew a light background print A Square to a gold print A Square. Sew pair of squares to light background print B Rectangle. (**Diagram 10**)

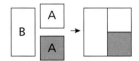

Diagram 10

2. Sew a rose C Diamond and a rose C reversed Diamond together; repeat two more times. Sew a dark green/brown print C and C reversed Diamonds together. (**Diagram 11**) Press the pieced diamond seams open as you go.

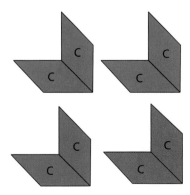

Diagram 11

Note: *Review the technique for Sewing Inset Seams, page 161.*

3. Sew the unit from step 1 to a pair of rose Diamonds from step 2. Sew a light background print F Square to remaining pairs of rose C Diamonds. Sew a light background print F Square to dark green/brown print C Diamond pair, leaving the corner seams open where the light background print F Square meets the dark green/brown print C Diamonds, at the arrow. (**Diagram 12**)

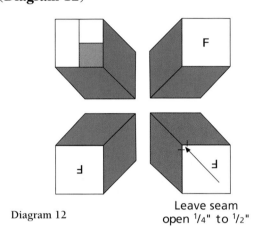

Diagram 12

Leave seam open ¼" to ½"

Tip: *When joining appliqué stems to patchwork sometimes you will need to leave a seam open just enough to tuck the appliqué under the patchwork. On the wrong side of the work, tack the appliqué and patchwork together in the seam.*

4. Stitch the four light background print G Triangles to the sides of the completed pieces. (**Diagram 13**)

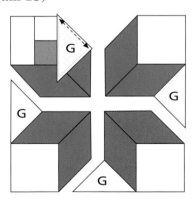

Diagram 13

5. Sew two flower sections together; repeat. Then sew the flower halves together beginning to

stitch from the center toward the outside edges. (**Diagram 14**)

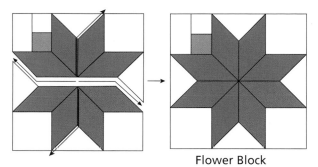

Flower Block

Diagram 14

6. Repeat steps 1 to 5 for 11 more Flower blocks.

Putting the Quilt Center Together

1. Lay out the completed Flower blocks and four light background J Rectangles. Pay close attention to the direction of the flower centers and the leaves. (**Diagram 15**)

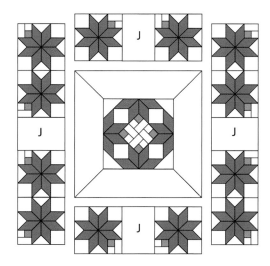

Diagram 15

2. Sew the blocks and J Rectangles together in strips. Sew the strips to the pieced center.

Flower Buds

Note: *Use the same techniques for sewing diamonds and setting in squares and triangles to assemble the Triangle Bud units.*

1. Referring to **Diagram 16**, sew a medium back-

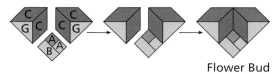

Flower Bud

Diagram 16

ground print A to a gold print A; sew to a medium background print B. Sew a rose C to a dark green/brown print C reversed; sew a medium background G triangle in between diamonds. Sew a rose C reversed to a dark green/brown print C. Sew units together.

2. Repeat step 1 and make 11 more Flower buds.

3. Sew an H Triangle to each dark green/brown print C Diamond to complete Triangle Flower Buds. Make four. Sew an H Triangle to a dark green/brown print C Diamond. Repeat three more times. Then, sew an H Triangle to the dark green/brown print C Diamond reversed. Repeat three more times. (**Diagram 17**)

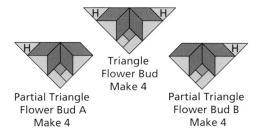

Triangle Flower Bud Make 4

Partial Triangle Flower Bud A Make 4

Partial Triangle Flower Bud B Make 4

Diagram 17

Making the Pieced Flower Bud Border

1. Referring to **Diagram 18**, assemble the pieced border strips using the Flower Buds, Partial Flower Buds A and B, eight light background print K Triangles, and eight light background print L Triangles. Make four border strips.

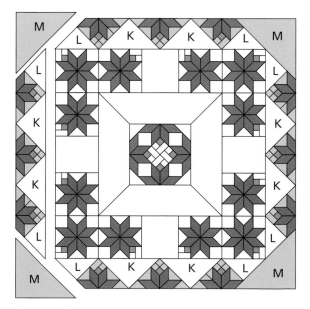

Diagram 18

31

2. Pin the strips to the center of the quilt matching the tips of Triangle Buds to where the blocks are sewn together. Sew a border strip to each side of the pieced center. Add a medium background print M Triangle at each corner.

Finishing the Quilt

Note: *Read Finishing Up, pages 161 to 174, to complete your quilt.*

1. Cut four medium background strips, 2½" x 31" and four border stripe fabric strips 3½" x 38". These measurements include the seam allowances. Mark the ¼" seam allowance along the long sides of the pieces. **Note:** *Measure your quilt and adjust border strip lengths if necessary.*

2. Add borders referring to Mitered Borders, page 165.

3. Referring to Appliqué Quilts, pages 147 to 155, prepare all leaves for appliqué and create the bias for stems.

4. Trace the Border Vine Placement (page 35) and Center Vine Placement (page 36) for appliqué onto freezer paper and cut out. Place the placement patterns onto the quilt top and pin or lightly press in place. Lightly mark around the paper patterns.

Note: *The Vine Placements are suggestions. Don't worry if your design deviates some from the original. Try to make the layout as symmetrical as possible.*

5. Baste the bias stems in place tucking ends in openings left in step 3 of Flower Blocks on page 30. Baste the leaves in place.

6. Using matching thread, appliqué the stems and leaves in place.

7. Using black embroidery floss, stitch around the flower centers using a Blanket stitch. (**Diagram 19**)

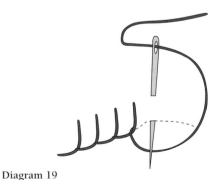

Diagram 19

8. Trace the quilting designs from page 37 onto freezer paper and cut out. Position the designs as needed and pin in place. Draw around the designs with an erasable marker. Use the Full Flower Quilting Pattern in the open areas on the light background and the Partial Flower Quilting Pattern in the triangle areas. (**Diagram 20**)

Diagram 20

9. Layer the quilt top, batting and backing together with the wrong sides of the quilt top and backing facing the batting. Baste or pin the layers together. Hand quilt.

10. Finish the quilt with continuous binding. Add a label on the quilt back.

Flowers of Friendship Quilt Layout

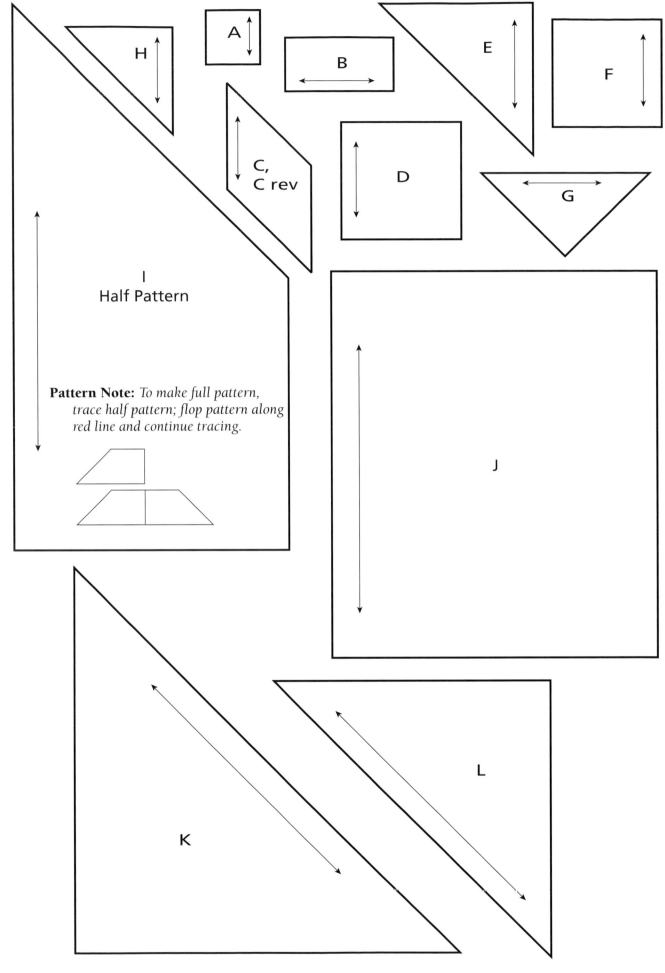

A

B

C,
C rev

D

E

F

G

H

I
Half Pattern

Pattern Note: *To make full pattern, trace half pattern; flop pattern along red line and continue tracing.*

J

K

L

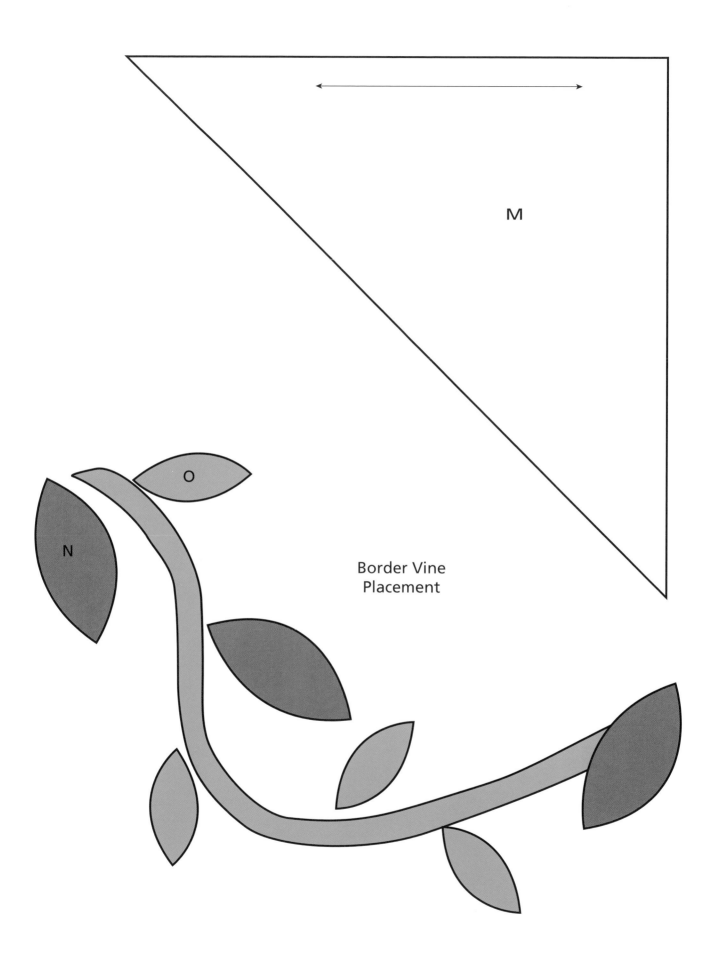

M

Border Vine
Placement

N

O

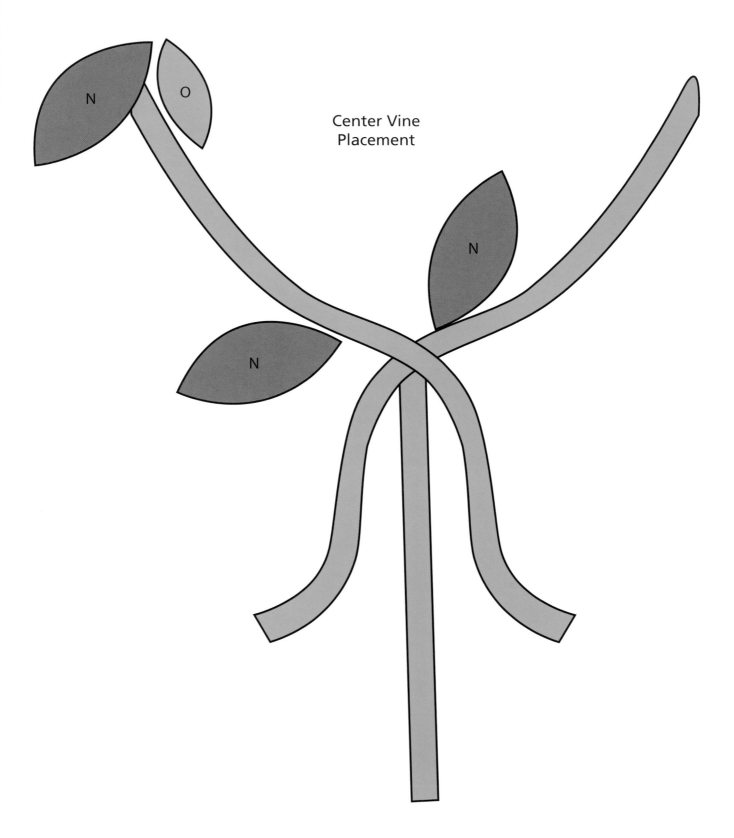

Center Vine
Placement

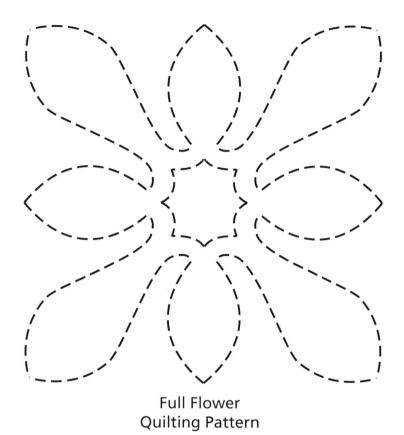

Full Flower
Quilting Pattern

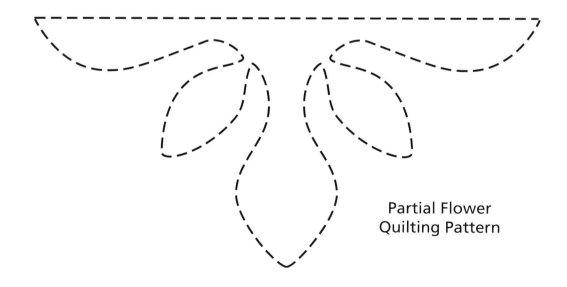

Partial Flower
Quilting Pattern

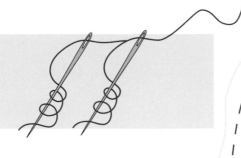

BIRDS IN THE AIR STARS

Approximate Size
59" x 75"

Block Size
4" x 4" finished

Notes: *Please read the General Directions, pages 142 to 174, before you begin. Fabric quantities specified are for 42" - 44" wide, 100% cotton fabrics. Templates **do not** include seam allowances. Strip-cut measurements **do** include seam allowances. Use a ¼" seam allowance. Sew with right sides together. Press seams as you go.*

Materials
Blocks
2 yards tan print
2½ yards beige
2 yards dark blue star print

Finishing
²/₃ yard beige with blue print (first border)
²/₃ yard dark blue star print (second border)
63" x 79" batting and backing

Patterns
A, B, C (page 42)

Cutting
Birds in the Air Blocks
432 A, beige
864 A, tan print
48 B, beige
96 B, dark blue star print
48 C, dark blue star print

Finishing
6 strips, 3½" x width of fabric, beige with blue print (first border)
6 strips, 3½" x width of fabric, dark blue star print (second border)

There are twelve large stars in this antique quilt. The pattern is called a composite design – one large design motif, the Star, is made up of many smaller elements. In this case each large star is composed of twelve four-inch, Birds in the Air Blocks. It must have been a special quilt to the original owner because it shows little wear.

Design Tip

Many patchwork blocks work well as single units placed side by side to create larger more complex designs – like the Birds in the Air Block. The Star, made by this block, is an excellent example of a composite design.

There are many ways to put the Birds in the Air Blocks together. On page 43, you can see a setting for 80 blocks arranged in what is commonly called a "Trip Around the World" setting.

Using the same size blocks and the same number and width of borders you can make a quilt 44" x 52".

Instructions

Preparing the Pieces

1. Make plastic templates for A, B, and C. Label the templates with all notations.

2. Trace templates on the wrong side of the fabrics according to the amounts and fabrics in Cutting on page 39.

Piecing the Birds in the Air Blocks

1. Sew a beige A Triangle to a tan print A Triangle. Repeat for three more pairs of A Triangles. (**Diagram 1**)

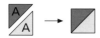

Diagram 1

2. For row 1, sew two triangle squares and a tan print A Triangle together. (**Diagram 2**)

Diagram 2

3. For row 2, sew a triangle square and a tan print A Triangle together. (**Diagram 3**)

Diagram 3

4. Sew rows 1 and 2 together. Sew tan print A Triangle to bottom of row 2 to complete a pieced triangle. (**Diagram 4**) Make 144 pieced triangles.

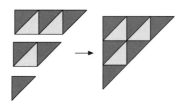

Diagram 4

5. Sew pieced unit from step 4 to a beige B Triangle. (**Diagram 5**) Make 48 light Birds in the Air blocks.

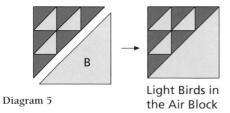

Diagram 5

Light Birds in the Air Block

6. Sew pieced unit from step 4 to a dark blue B Triangle. (**Diagram 6**) Make 96 dark Birds in the Air blocks.

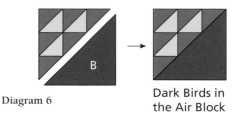

Diagram 6

Dark Birds in the Air Block

Assembling the Star Blocks

1. Sew a dark blue C Square to a dark Birds in the Air block. Sew a dark Birds in the Air block to a light Birds in the Air block. Sew pairs of blocks together. (**Diagram 7**) Repeat three more times.

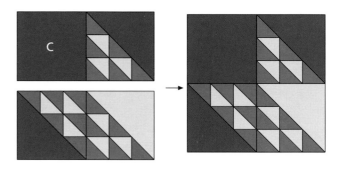

Diagram 7

Tip: *Pay attention to the direction of the center beige triangles – it's easy to spin this pinwheel the wrong way.*

2. Sew units from step 1 together to make a Star block. (**Diagram 8**) Make 12 Star blocks.

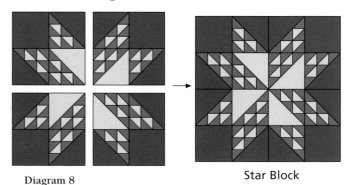

Diagram 8

Star Block

Finishing the Quilt

Note: *Read Finishing Up, pages 161 to 174, to complete your quilt.*

1. Lay out the twelve Star blocks in four rows of three blocks. Sew together by hand or machine.

2. Sew 3½"-wide beige with blue print strips together into one long strip. Measure quilt lengthwise. Cut two strips to that length and sew to sides of quilt. Measure quilt crosswise and cut two strips to that length. Sew to top and bottom of quilt.

3. Repeat step 1 with the 3½"-wide dark blue star print strips for the second border.

4. Layer the quilt top, batting and backing together with the wrong sides of the quilt top and backing facing the batting. Baste or pin the layers together.

5. Quilt as desired.

6. Trim backing and batting even with quilt top.

7. Finish the edge of the quilt by turning the dark blue star print border fabric toward the back and stitching down.

8. Add a label to the quilt back.

Birds in the Air Stars Quilt Layout

41

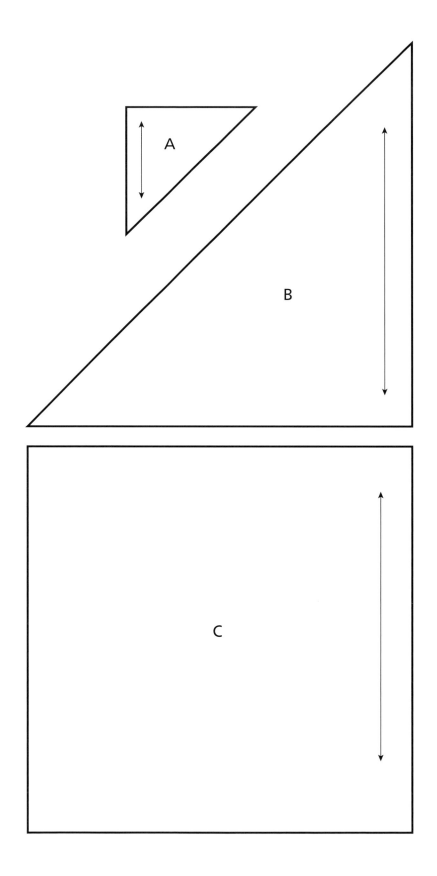

A

B

C

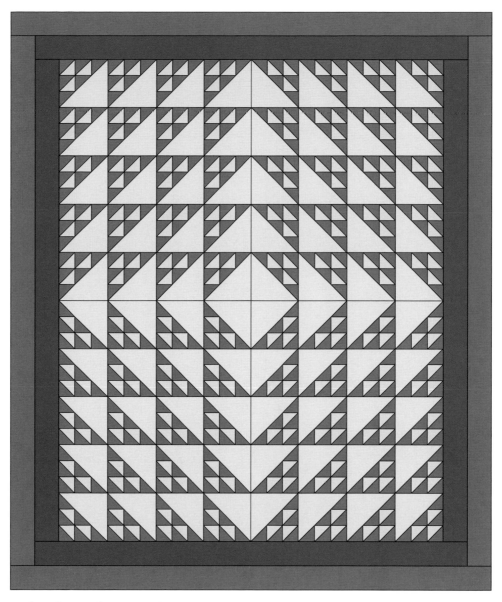

Birds in the Air Alternate Quilt Layout

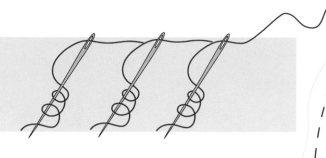

Prickly Pear Medallion

Approximate Size

42½" x 42½"

Block Size

12" x 12" finished

Notes: *Please read the General Directions, pages 142 to 174, before you begin. Fabric quantities specified are for 42" - 44" wide, 100% cotton. Templates **do not** include seam allowances. Strip-cut measurements **do** include seam allowances. Sew with right sides together. Press seams as you go.*

Materials

Hints: *This quilt uses striped fabric. Stripe fabric adds extra interest to a quilt, but using it requires extra attention to details.*

Blocks
⅓ yard red
⅓ yard light green
⅓ yard black
¼ yard pink
1⅓ yards border stripe print (or ¾ yard dark print fabric)

Finishing
1⅓ yards backing and batting
⅓ yard binding

Patterns

Note: *Trace and cut out all templates.*

Prickly Pear block A, B, C (page 51)
D triangle (page 51)
E border (page 51)
F triangle (page 51)
G square (page 51)
I triangle (page 53)
J triangle (page 53)
K square (page 53)

Note: *Templates H and L (page 52) are made from strips cut on page 46.*

This classic medallion-style pieced quilt is easier than it looks. The central block sets the design theme for the quilt. The other design elements are all related to the center focal point - the Prickly Pear Cactus block.

Making a Harmonious Medallion Design

There is a lot going on in this quilt but it remains a unified concept. The principle block, Prickly Pear, is set on point, diagonally, in the center of the quilt. The design elements from the central block continue to the edge of the quilt in a series of square-in-square designs and repeating half-square triangle motifs. A careful look at the repetition of shapes and colored fabrics provide additional unifying design concepts.

Cutting

Prickly Pear

36 A Triangles, red
4 B Squares, red
28 F Triangles, red
24 J Triangles, red
36 A Triangles, light green
28 F Triangles, light green
24 J Triangles, light green
12 B Squares, black
4 D Triangles, black
4 G Squares, black
8 J Triangles, black
4 K Squares, black
8 C Triangles, pink
4 I Triangles, pink
1 B Square, border stripe
8 C Triangles, border stripe
8 E Borders, border stripe

Finishing

12 strips, $4\frac{1}{8}$" x $22\frac{7}{8}$", border stripe (4 H and 8 L)
5 strips, $2\frac{1}{4}$"-wide, border stripe (binding)

Instructions

Making the Prickly Pear Blocks

1. Review General Directions for Hand Piecing Techniques including Sewing Inset Seams, pages 158 to 161.

2. Lay out Prickly Pear Block pieces. (**Diagram 1**) **Note:** *Layout on a piece of flannel or batting so the pieces don't shift.*

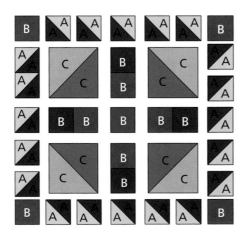

Diagram 1

3. To begin, sew a light green A Triangle and a red A Triangle together. (**Diagram 2**) Repeat 35 more times for a total of 36 triangle squares.

Diagram 2

4. Set aside four light green/red triangle squares, then sew remaining light green/red triangle squares together in pairs. (**Diagram 3**)

Diagram 3

5. Sew a pink C Triangle and a border stripe C Triangle together. (**Diagram 4**) Repeat seven more times.

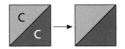

Diagram 4

6. Sew a pair of A triangle squares to a C triangle square; sew a black B Square to a pair of A triangle squares. Sew units together. (**Diagram 5**) Repeat seven more times for a total of eight A/B/C units.

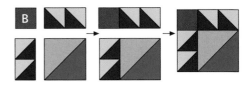

Diagram 5

7. Set aside four of the A/B/C units made in step 6.

8. Sew a black B Square and a red B Square together; sew to a light green/red A triangle square. Note position of A triangle square. (**Diagram 6**) Repeat three more times.

Diagram 6

9. Sew an A/B/C unit to opposite sides A/B/B unit; repeat. Sew an A/B/B unit to opposite sides of a border stripe B Square. Sew units together to make Prickly Pear center. (**Diagram 7**)

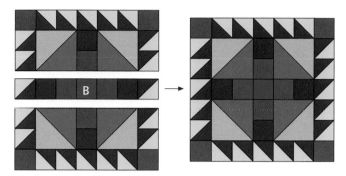

Diagram 7

10. Press and check to make sure the block measures 12½" x 12½".

Note: *Remember, the block at this stage will include a ½" seam allowance.*

Creating the Medallion

1. Sew a border stripe E Border to a black D Triangle. (**Diagram 8**)

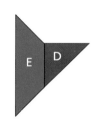

Diagram 8

2. Sew another border stripe E to adjacent side of black D Triangle; sew diagonal seam of E Borders, sewing from center out. (**Diagram 9**)

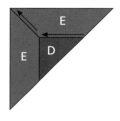

Diagram 9

3. Sew D/E triangle units to Prickly Pear center. (**Diagram 10**)

Diagram 10

4. Sew a light green F triangle and a red F triangle together. (**Diagram 11**) Repeat 27 more times for a total of 28 F triangle squares.

Diagram 11

5. Sew seven F triangle squares together. (**Diagram 12**) Repeat three more times.

Diagram 12

6. Sew an F triangle square unit from step 5 to opposite sides of Prickly Pear center. (**Diagram 13**)

Diagram 13

7. Sew a black G Square to opposite sides of remaining F triangle units and sew to Prickly Pear center. (**Diagram 14**)

Diagram 14

8. Using a 45-degree angle, cut the corners off of the 4⅛" x 22⅞" dark border stripe strips. These pieces are the correct measurements and include the seam allowances. Mark the ¼" seam allowance inside each edge of the fabric using the pattern on page 52. Four of the strips are H Borders and eight are L Borders.

9. Sew the H Borders to all sides of the center. Press the seams toward the edge. (**Diagram 15**)

Diagram 15

10. Sew the pink I Triangles to the center to fill in the corners. (**Diagram 16**)

Diagram 16

11. Sew a light green J Triangle to a red J Triangle. (**Diagram 17**) Repeat 23 more times for a total of 24 J triangle squares.

Diagram 17

12. Sew three J triangle squares together; sew a black J Triangle to one end. Repeat, except sew black J Triangle to opposite end. (**Diagram 18**)

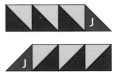

Diagram 18

13. Sew units from step 12 to lower edges of an A/B/C unit. (**Diagram 19**) Repeat three more times.

Diagram 19

14. Sew strips just made to opposite sides of quilt center. (**Diagram 20**)

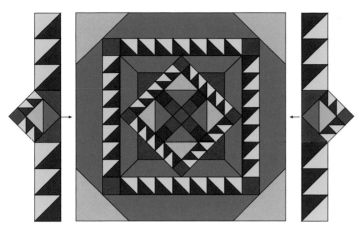

Diagram 20

15. Sew a black K Square to opposite ends of remaining strips from step 12. (**Diagram 21**)

Diagram 21

16. Sew remaining borders to top and bottom of quilt center. (**Diagram 22**)

Diagram 22

17. Sew L Borders (step 8) to all sides; set in the diagonal seams. (**Diagram 23**)

Diagram 23

Finishing the Quilt

Note: *Read Finishing Up, pages 161 to 174, to complete your quilt.*

1. Layer the quilt top, batting and backing together with the wrong sides of the quilt top facing the batting. Baste or pin the layers in place. Hand quilt in straight lines following the pieced patterns.

2. Finish the edge of the quilt with continuous binding. Add a label to the quilt back.

Prickly Pear Medallion Quilt Layout

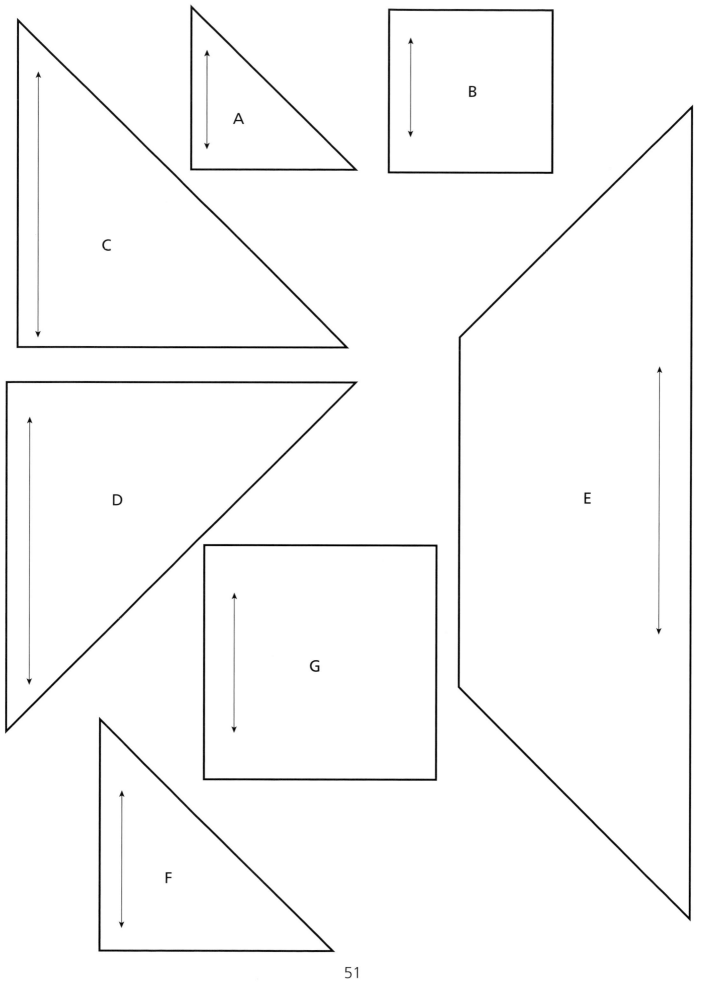

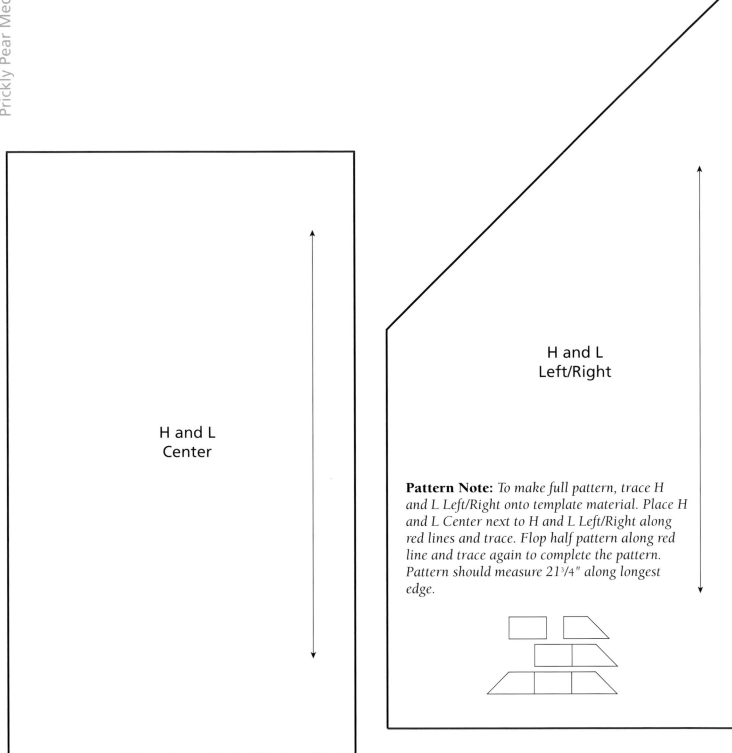

H and L
Center

H and L
Left/Right

Pattern Note: *To make full pattern, trace H and L Left/Right onto template material. Place H and L Center next to H and L Left/Right along red lines and trace. Flop half pattern along red line and trace again to complete the pattern. Pattern should measure 21³/4" along longest edge.*

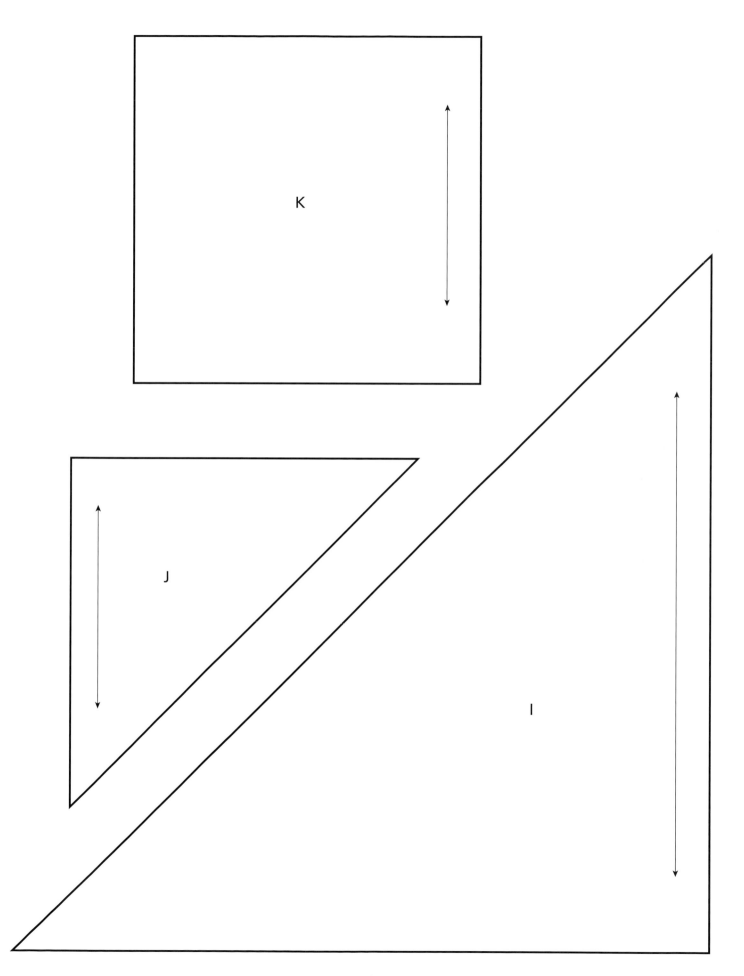

K

J

I

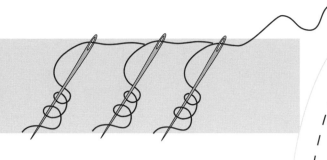

Red Nine-Patch

Approximate Size
72" x 80"

Block Size
4½" x 4½" finished

Notes: *Please read the General Directions, pages 142 to 174, before you begin. Fabric quantities specified are for 42" - 44" wide, 100% cotton. Templates **do not** include seam allowances. Strip-cut measurements **do** include seam allowances. Sew with right sides together. Press seams as you go.*

Materials
Pieced Blocks

2 yards muslin or other light solid
1½ yards dark prints (If using scraps, you will need five 2" squares from each scrap fabric for each block.)

Finishing

2 yards red (setting blocks and triangles)
1 yard muslin or other light (first border)
2 yards red (second border, binding)
5 yards backing
76" x 84" batting

Patterns
Note: *Make templates A and B.*

A square (page 59)
B square (page 59)
C Triangle (page 59)
D Triangle (page 59)

The quiltmaking language of the Nine-Patch is easy to understand. It consists of three rows of three pieces each. The pieces can be simple squares or the pieces can be of more complicated designs. The Nine-Patch is basic to the quiltmaking experience. Because it is a fundamental block, it lends itself to beginning quiltmakers for its ease of construction and to more advanced quiltmakers for experimenting with more complicated piecing like the Shoo-Fly quilt, page 122. This quilt will challenge your scrap basket. There are 90 Nine-Patch Blocks set together on the diagonal—nine blocks by ten blocks. The old Nine-Patch blocks were collected and placed in a modern setting with two borders.

Cutting

Blocks

Notes: *Trace around Template A onto the muslin and dark print fabrics. Mark the corners clearly. Trace the number of pieces you need for the quilt. Use 360 muslin and 450 dark. Cut pieces leaving about a ¼" seam allowance around each side.*

360 A squares, muslin (Nine-Patch blocks)
450 A squares, dark prints (Nine-Patch blocks)

Reminder: *For accuracy, place the right side of the fabric over a piece of fine sandpaper then trace around the template with a sharp, fine pencil. The sandpaper grips the fabric so that it doesn't shift under the pencil.*

Finishing

Notes: *Trace around Template B on the red fabric. Mark the corners clearly and pay close attention to the grain line notations on the template. Use Templates C and D to trace inside the fabric cut for the Setting and Corner triangles.*

72 B squares, red (Alternate squares)
9 squares, 8" x 8", red (Cut in quarters on the diagonal for setting triangles.)
2 squares, 5" x 5", red (Cut in half on the diagonal for corner triangles.)
12 strips, 2" x width of fabric, muslin (first border and binding)
8 strips 6" x width of fabric, red (second border)

Instructions

Making the Blocks

1. Lay out all the pieces for one block. Pay close attention to where the muslin and dark squares are in relation to each other. (**Diagram 1**)

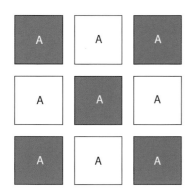

Diagram 1

2. Carefully pin and sew each square together in rows. (**Diagram 2**)

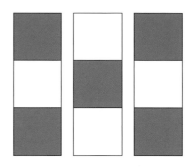

Diagram 2

3. Assemble the strips to create the Nine-Patch Block. Make 90 Nine-Patch Blocks. (**Diagram 3**)

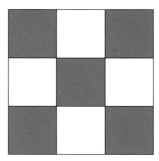

Diagram 3

Finishing the Quilt

Note: *Read Finishing Up, pages 161 to 174, to complete your quilt.*

1. Lay out the Nine-Patch blocks in diagonal rows. Place the Setting Triangles and Corner Triangles as illustrated. (**Diagram 4**)

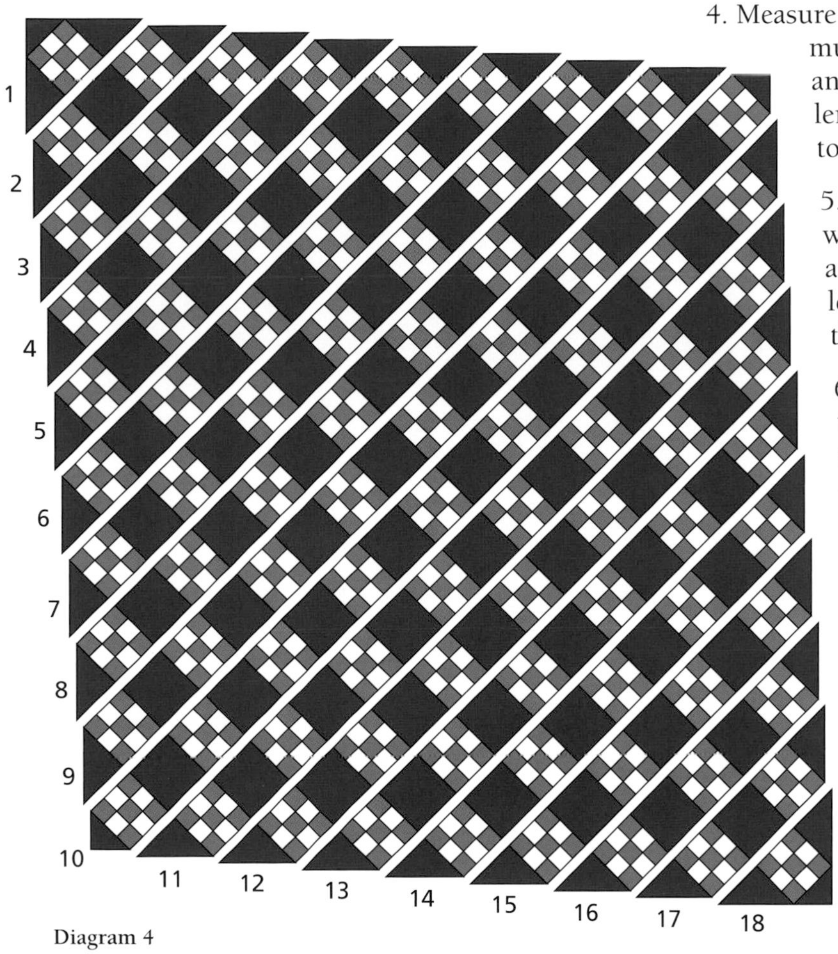

Diagram 4

2. Carefully pin and piece the body of the quilt together on the diagonal in strips. Assemble the strips to complete quilt. Check off each row as you complete it and label each row.

HINT: *As you complete the diagonal rows keep them numbered/labeled and in sequence.*

3. Sew the diagonal rows together in sequence.

4. Measure the quilt crosswise. Cut two 2"-wide muslin strips to that length. Sew to the top and bottom of the quilt. Measure the quilt lengthwise. Cut two 2"-wide muslin strips to that length. Sew to sides of quilt.

5. Measure the quilt crosswise. Cut two 6"-wide red strips to that length. Sew to top and bottom of quilt. Measure the quilt lengthwise. Cut two 6"-wide red strips to that length. Sew to sides of quilt.

6. Layer the quilt top, batting and backing together with the wrong sides of the quilt top and backing facing the batting. Baste or pin the layers together. Hand quilt your quilt.

7. Finish the edge of the quilt with continuous binding. Add a label to the quilt back.

Note: *The final border is quilted with a simple cable design. Mark the corner design at the corners of the quilt. Fill in the remaining cables along the sides, top and bottom of the quilt. The length of some of those cables may need to be adjusted to fit.*

Red Nine-Patch Quilt Layout

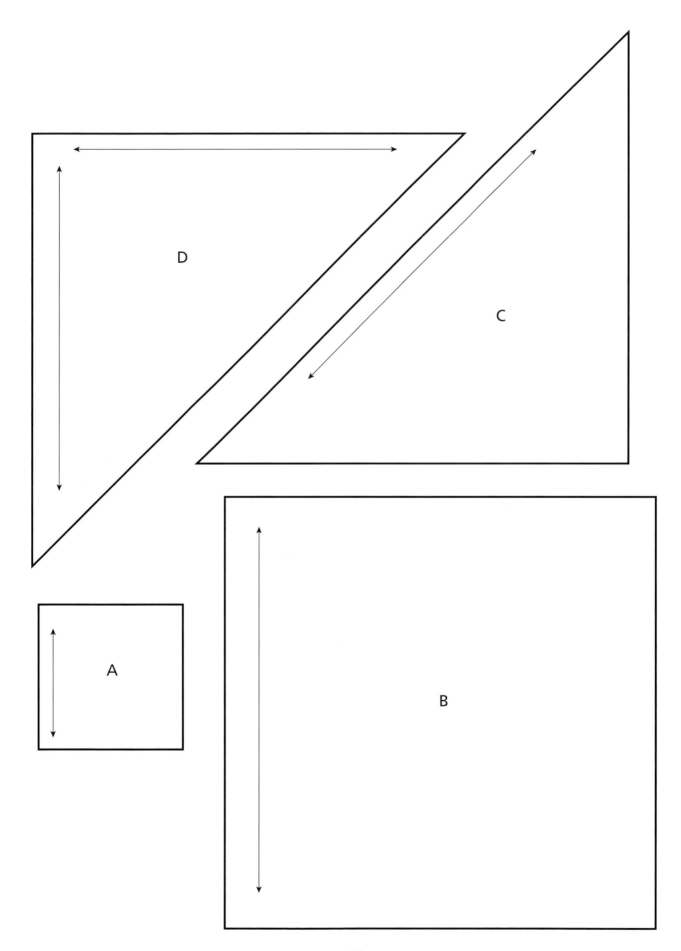

Star Studded

Approximate Size
33" x 57¾"

Star Block Size
2¾" x 2¾" finished

Materials

Blocks
1¾ yards total, assorted medium/dark print fabric scraps for stars
1¾ yards total assorted light background fabrics
Template plastic

Finishing
1 yard blue
40" x 67" backing fabric

Patterns
Star A, B, C, D (page 63)
Square E (page 63)

Cutting
Note: *Make templates for A, B, C, D, E. Do **not** include seam allowances. Mark around each template on the wrong side of the fabric. Remember to allow about ½" around each tracing to allow for the seam allowance. Cut each piece from the fabric with a ¼" seam allowance.*

For Each Star, cut:
4 A Triangles, light background
4 C Squares, light background
8 B Triangles, medium/dark prints
1 D Square, medium/dark prints

Finishing
112 E Squares, blue

Rescued in the last quarter of the twentieth century, this quilt is a piece of cot bedding. It is not quilted, but tied together without an inner-lining or batting. It is most likely for a wagon cot or for a child's bed. The style of the quilt, the fabrics, and the colors assist us in dating the quilt as being made in the last quarter of the nineteenth century.

The backing is a shirting print of the period on a white background. The lighter fabrics within the star blocks are different, but of similar types. The small figures are in stiff, regimented rows, grids, or stripes. The scraps of fabrics in the stars are varied and often pieced together to make the scraps large enough to create the star. This is astonishing when one is reminded that the star size is only 2¾" square. The blue squares that complete the setting design are all the same fabric. Fragile fabrics have been conserved by hand stitching silk tulle over the broken fabric fragments.

At a time in the history of the quilt when we have no need to warm ourselves with coverings made from bits and pieces left from clothing construction or from the remaining fragments left of a used garment, we still treasure the rare quilt that has survived a hundred or more years. We marvel at the industry and artistry of this anonymous quiltmaker. By making replica quilts, we honor the talents of earlier quiltmakers.

At present, our interest in quiltmaking tends to be an expression of artistic talent. In a similar way, a painter can work with color from a tube or paint box, the modern quilter can choose from any color palette. Whether you choose to opt for your own palette to recreate this small quilt or choose to replicate the original look with modern fabrics you will be paying tribute to an unknown quiltmaker.

Instructions

Making the Block

1. Lay out the pieces for a Star Block. (**Diagram 1**)

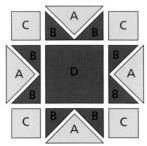

Diagram 1

2. Sew two medium/dark print B triangles to a light background A triangle. (**Diagram 2**) Repeat three more times.

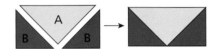

Diagram 2

3. Sew a light background C square to opposite sides of an A/B unit; repeat. Sew an A/B unit to opposite sides of a medium print D square. Sew rows together. (**Diagram 3**)

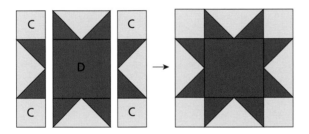

Diagram 3

4. When you have pieced five Star Blocks, combine them with four blue squares to create one Master Block. Sew the blue squares and Star Blocks first into rows and then sew rows together. This block will finish at 8¼" square. (**Diagram 4**)

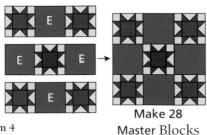

Diagram 4

Make 28
Master Blocks

Finishing the Quilt

1. Lay out seven rows with four Master Blocks in each row. Piece together each row. Join the individual rows. The blue squares will appear to be sashing. (**Diagram 5**)

Diagram 5

2. Place quilt top and backing right sides together. Sew along all four sides using a ¼" seam allowance and leaving an opening large enough for turning. Turn quilt right side out through opening, then sew opening closed. **Note:** *Refer to pages 169 to 171 if you prefer to layer the quilt with batting and hand quilt.*

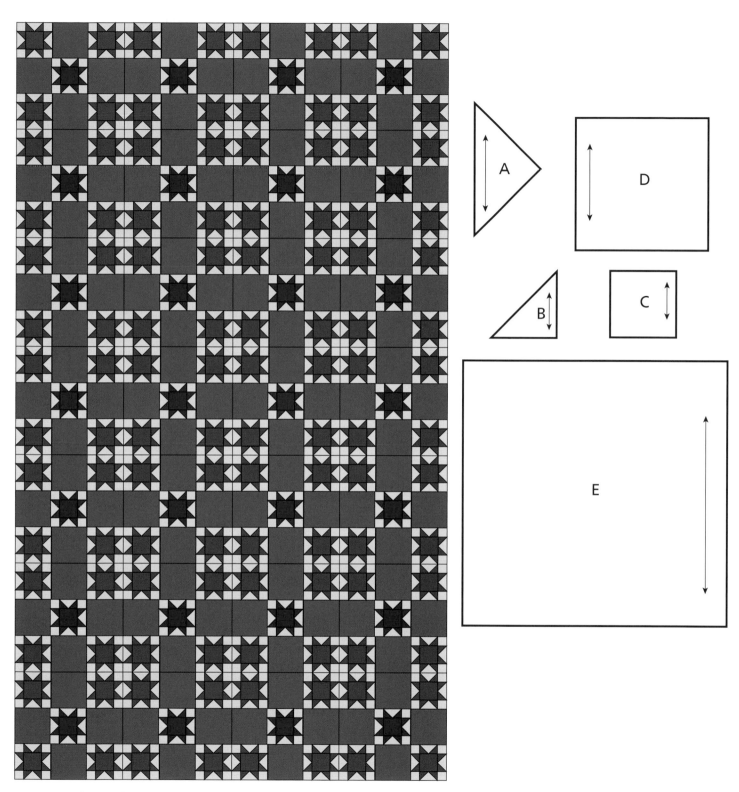

Star Studded Quilt Layout

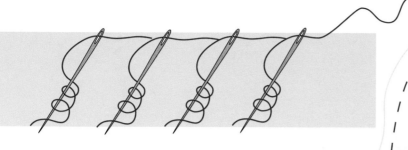

Comet Catcher

Approximate Size
22½" x 22½"

Notes: *Please read the General Directions, pages 142 to 174, before you begin. Fabric quantities specified are for 42" - 44" wide, 100% cotton fabrics. Templates **do not** include seam allowances. Strip-cut measurements **do** include seam allowances. Use a ¼" seam allowance. Sew with right sides together. Press seams as you go.*

Material
Block
¾ yard dark blue print (Crescents, border and binding)
1 fat quarter yellow (Crescents)
1 fat quarter gold (background)
Freezer paper
Glue stick

Finishing
1 fat eighth (9" x 11") blue plaid (cornerstones)
¾ yard backing
25" x 25" batting

Pattern
Note: *Make a plastic template of the Crescent shape. Label the template with all notations.*

Quilting Pattern (page 68)
Crescent (page 69)

Cutting
Block
6 crescents, dark blue print
6 crescents, yellow
1 square, 16½" x 16½", gold (block background)

Finishing
4 squares, 3½" x 3½", blue plaid (cornerstones)
4 rectangles, 3½" x 16½", dark blue print (border)
3 strips, 2½"-wide x width of fabric, dark blue print (binding)

The Comet Catcher quilt is a good marriage of fabric with a theme or conversation print in celestial designs and quilt pattern. Any number of similar fabrics would carry the theme or title of the quilt as easily as the fabric that is used.
Consider the difference the fabric makes in this quilt and in the larger version of the pattern the Windblown Daisy quilt, page 70.

Using Conversation Prints

Conversation Prints are fabric designs that feature recognizable objects as the print motif. Sometimes the prints are called "object prints."

Conversation prints have been manufactured in America from the mid-1800s to the current day. They are fun to use and can add interest and value to the appropriate style quilt design.

Instructions

Making the Block

1. Lay yellow and dark blue print fabrics wrong side up. Position the Crescent template so that you can read the "TSU" notation (This Side Up). Trace around the template six times onto each fabric fat quarter. Mark the "stop-stitching-here" notch. Allow at least $1/2$" between all traced lines. This is a reversing shape so take care to mark all the Crescent pieces in the same direction.

2. Cut Crescents from the fabrics making sure to leave a $1/4$" seam allowance around each traced line.

3. Pick up one yellow and one dark blue Crescent and place right sides together. With the wrong side of the yellow Crescent facing up, place a pin through the point at the end with the "X" mark, through the right side of the dark blue Crescent at the end marked with the "X". (**Diagram 1**)

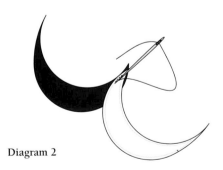

Diagram 1

4. Stitch about a $1/4$" toward the end point; reverse and start piecing along the length of the crescent. Remove pin. (**Diagram 2**)

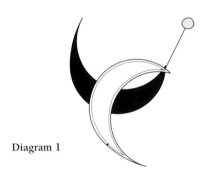

Diagram 2

5. Continue stitching along the crescent curve. (**Diagram 3**)

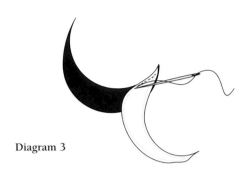

Diagram 3

Hint: *Check each side of the seam to make sure you are stitching on the seam line of each piece. Check yourself every two or three stitches. This is an extreme curve to piece. It is easier to stitch these curves by hand and with only the one pin at the beginning. Stop stitching the crescent curve at the marked notch. The curve will extend about three inches beyond the pieced seam. Carefully clip along the pieced seam.*

6. Pick up a dark crescent and repeat the piecing steps. Press along the curved seams. (**Diagram 4**)

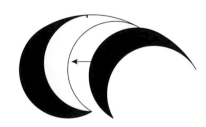

Diagram 4

7. Complete two units of three Crescents with the dark blue on the outside and two units of three crescents with yellow on the outside. (**Diagram 5**)

Diagram 5

8. Join all units. Press carefully. (**Diagram 6**)

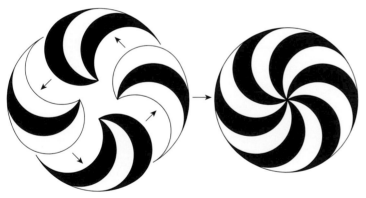

Diagram 6

9. Measure the size of the Crescent circle from the marked seam lines. It will vary some, but it should be about $12\frac{1}{2}$" in diameter. Cut a circle this size from the freezer paper.

10. Place the pieced Crescent circle on a flat ironing surface with the wrong side up. Place the freezer paper circle down on the fabric with the shiny side down. The paper circle should fit along the seam allowance edges of the fabric circle. Press

freezer paper to the Crescent circle. Run the glue stick around the edge of the paper. Fold the fabric seam allowance over the paper and stick in place to create a clean edge on the right side of the fabric circle. (**Diagram 7**)

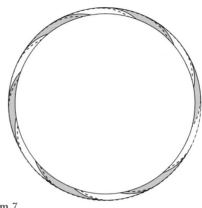

Diagram 7

11. Fold the gold background square into quarters and press. (**Diagram 8**)

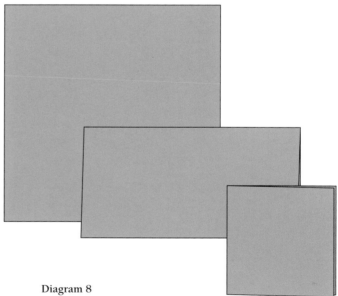

Diagram 8

12. Center the Crescent circle over the right side of the background fabric and pin in place. (**Diagram 9**)

Diagram 9

13. Appliqué the circle to the background square. Remove freezer paper referring to Appliqué Quilts, pages 147 to 155.

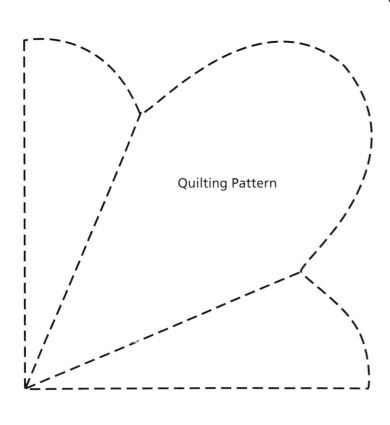

Quilting Pattern

Finishing the Quilt

Note: *Read Finishing Up, pages 161 to 174, to complete your quilt.*

1. Sew 3½" x 16½" dark blue print rectangles to the top and bottom of the block. Sew 3½" blue plaid corner squares to the ends of the two remaining rectangles and stitch these to the block. (**Diagram 10**)

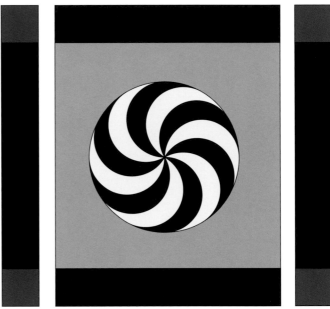

Diagram 10

2. Mark the quilting pattern at the corners of the gold background square.

3. Layer the quilt top, batting and backing together with the wrong sides of the quilt top and backing facing the batting. Baste or pin the layers together. Quilt along the design and the patterns in the corners.

4. Finish the edge of the quilt with continuous binding. Add a label to the quilt back.

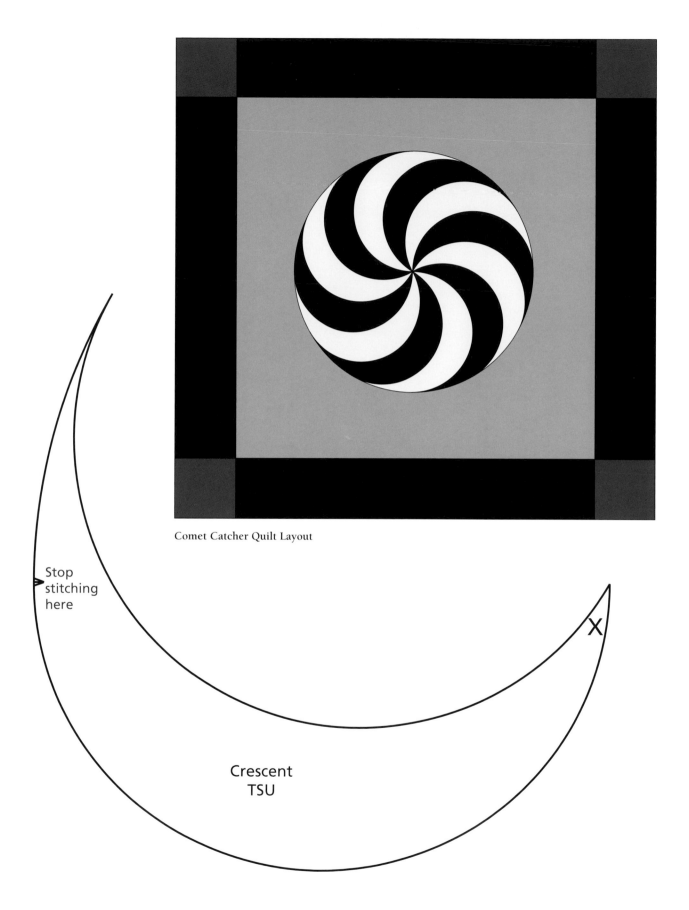

Comet Catcher Quilt Layout

Stop
stitching
here

X

Crescent
TSU

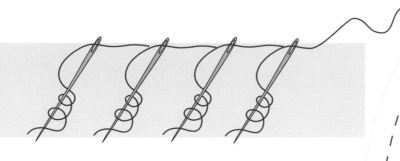

Windblown Daisy

Approximate Size
71" x 90"

Block Size
16" x 16" finished

Notes: *Please read the General Directions, pages 142 to 174, before you begin. Fabric quantities specified are for 42" - 44" wide, 100% cotton fabrics. Templates **do not** include seam allowances. Strip-cut measurements **do** include seam allowances. Use a 1/4" seam allowance. Sew with right sides together. Press seams as you go.*

Materials
Blocks
12 assorted fat quarters, light prints (Crescents)
12 assorted fat quarters, medium to dark prints (Crescents)
2³/4 yards red (background)
Glue stick
Freezer paper

Finishing
1³/4 yards brown plaid (sashing)
Fat quarter blue plaid (cornerstones)
3 yards red plaid (border)
³/4 yard light print (binding)
6 yards backing
76" x 96" batting

Patterns
Note: *Make a plastic template of the Crescent shape. Label the template with all notations.*

Crescent (page 77)
Quilting Pattern (page 77)

This quilt was collected from a second-hand store in Arizona towards the end of the twentieth century. Although the design was a popular one in both of the Carolinas from about the 1890s onward, it wasn't illustrated for common usage until designer Nancy Cabot captured the pattern and published it in 1933. The quilt top probably traveled west with its family and was quilted sometime in mid-twentieth century. After the quilt was purchased, additional hand quilting was added to the quilt and it was finally bound with the pre-cut and prepared straight-edge binding that was found and preserved with the quilt. Both the designer and original quiltmaker are anonymous.

The setting for this quilt is a simple one. It consists of twelve large blocks placed in sashing with cornerstones and surrounded by a wide border. The hallmark of the quilt is the circle of whirling crescents in the center of each block. Each circle is made up of twelve Crescents.

In the original quilt shown, the blocks are somewhat irregular and the border contains a second fabric. One wonders if the maker ran out of her first choice or some disaster overtook the missing red plaid border piece.

The measurements and the piecing instructions have been updated for the modern quiltmaker.

Cutting

Blocks

12 Squares, 16½" x 16½", red (background)
72 Crescents, light prints
72 Crescents, medium to dark prints

Finishing

6 squares, 3½" x 3½", blue plaid (cornerstones)
17 strips, 3½" x 16½", brown plaid (sashing)
2 strips, 3½" x 54½", brown plaid (top and bottom sashing)
2 strips, 3½" x 79½", brown plaid (side sashing)
4 strips (cut lengthwise), 6"-wide, red plaid (border)
9 strips, 2½"-wide by width of fabric, light print (binding)

Instructions

Making the Block

1. Lay all crescent fabric wrong side up. Position the Crescent template so that you can read the "TSU" notation (This Side Up). Trace around the template six times onto each fabric fat quarter. Mark the "stop-stitching-here" notch. Allow at least ½" between all traced lines. This is a reversing shape so take care to mark all the Crescent pieces in the same direction.

2. Cut crescents from the fabrics making sure to leave a ¼" seam allowance around each traced line.

3. Pick up one light and one dark Crescent and place right sides together. With the wrong side of the light Crescent facing up, place a pin through the point at the end with the "X" mark, and through the right side of the dark Crescent at the end marked with the "X". (**Diagram 1**)

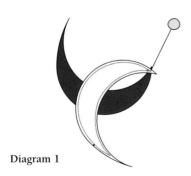

Diagram 1

4. Stitch about a ¼" toward the end point and reverse and start piecing along the length of the Crescent. Remove pin. (**Diagram 2**)

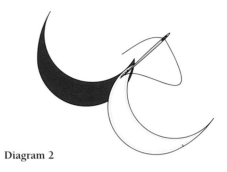

Diagram 2

5. Continue stitching along the Crescent curve. (**Diagram 3**)

Diagram 3

Hint: *Check each side of the seam to make sure you are stitching on the seam line of each piece. Check yourself every two or three stitches. This is an extreme curve to piece. It is easier to stitch these curves by hand and with only one pin at the beginning. Stop stitching the crescent curve at the mark. The curve will extend about three inches beyond the pieced seam. Carefully clip along the pieced seam.*

6. Pick up a dark Crescent and repeat the piecing steps. Press along the curved seams. (**Diagram 4**)

Diagram 4

7. Complete two units of three Crescents with the dark on the outside and two units of three Crescents with light on the outside. (**Diagram 5**)

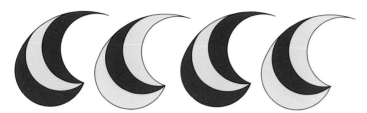

Diagram 5

8. Join all units. Press carefully. (**Diagram 6**)

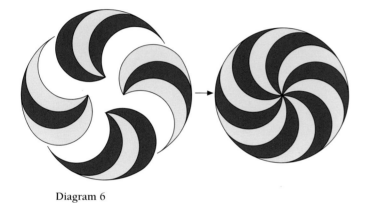

Diagram 6

9. Measure the size of the Crescent circle from the marked seam lines. It will vary some, but it should be about 12½" in diameter. Cut a circle this size from the freezer paper.

10. Place the pieced Crescent circle on a flat ironing surface with the wrong side up. Place the freezer paper circle down on the fabric with the shiny side down. The paper circle should fit along the seam allowance edges of the fabric circle. Press freezer paper to the Crescent circle. (**Diagram 7**)

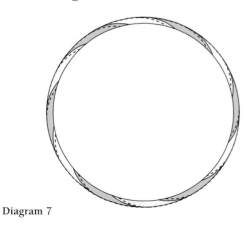

Diagram 7

11. Run the glue stick around the edge of the paper. Fold the fabric seam allowance over the paper and stick in place to create a clean edge on the right side of the fabric circle.

12. Fold the background square into quarters and press. (**Diagram 8**)

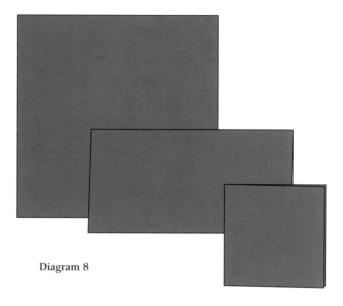

Diagram 8

13. Center the Crescent circle over the right side of the background fabric and pin in place. (**Diagram 9**)

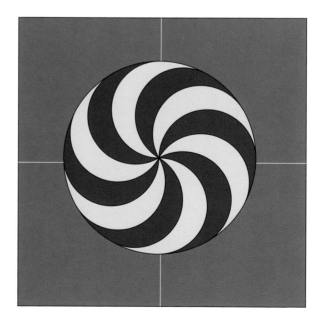

Diagram 9

73

14. Appliqué the circle to the background square. Remove freezer paper referring to Appliqué Quilts, pages147 to 155.

15. Repeat steps for all twelve blocks.

Finishing

Note: *Read Finishing Up, pages 161 to 174, and complete your quilt.*

1. Sew the $3\frac{1}{2}$" x $16\frac{1}{2}$" brown sashing strips to the blocks in four horizontal strips of three blocks. Sew three brown $3\frac{1}{2}$" x $16\frac{1}{2}$" sashing strips together with two $3\frac{1}{2}$" blue plaid squares set between them. (**Diagram 10**)

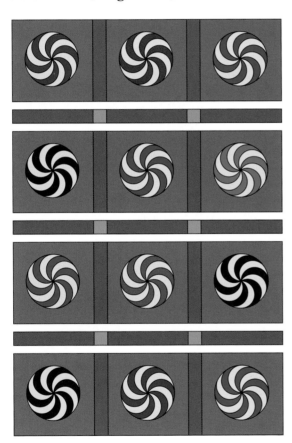

Diagram 10

2. Join the horizontal rows of blocks with the horizontal rows of sashing. Sew a $3\frac{1}{2}$" x $54\frac{1}{2}$" brown plaid strip to the top and bottom; sew the $3\frac{1}{2}$" x $79\frac{1}{2}$" brown plaid strips to the sides. (**Diagram 11**)

Diagram 11

3. For the border, measure the quilt crosswise. Cut two 6"-wide red plaid strips to that length. Sew to top and bottom of quilt. Measure the quilt lengthwise. Cut two 6"-wide red plaid strips to that length. Sew to sides of quilt.

4. Mark quilting pattern in corners of each block. (**Diagram 12**)

5. Layer the quilt top, batting and backing together with the wrong sides of the quilt top and backing facing the batting. Baste or pin the layers together. Quilt along the the marked pattern and crescent shapes.

6. Finish the edge of the quilt with continuous binding. Add a label to the quilt back.

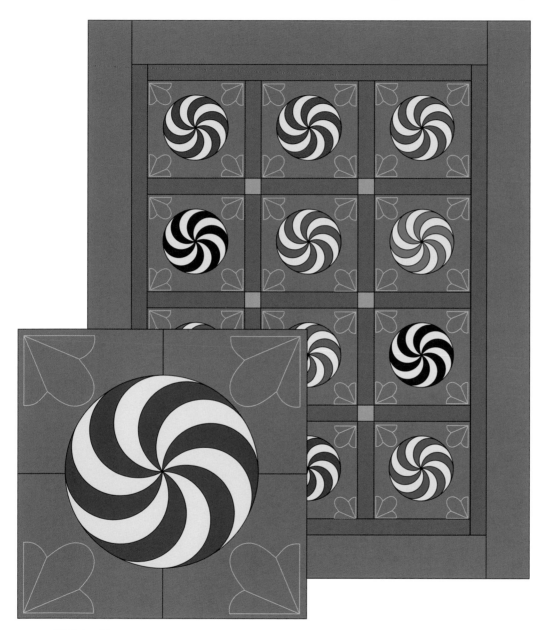

Diagram 12

75

Windblown Daisy Quilt Layout

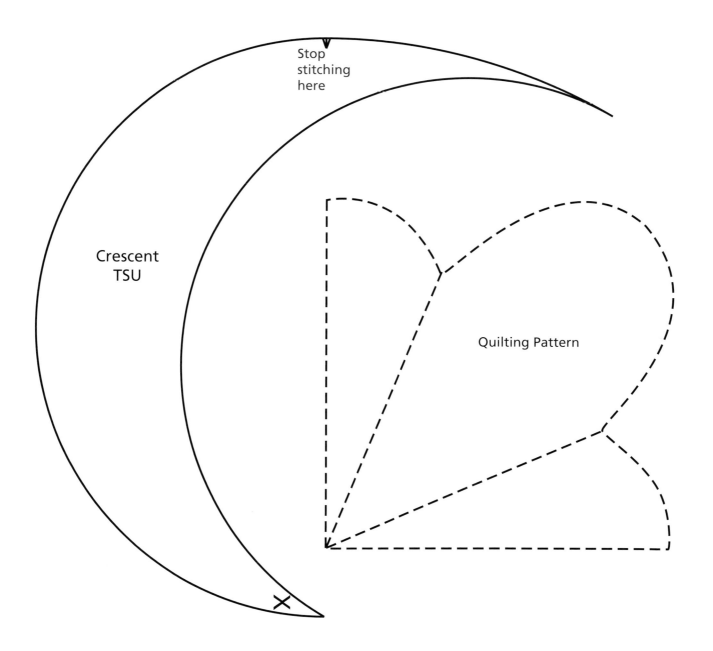

Stop
stitching
here

Crescent
TSU

Quilting Pattern

X

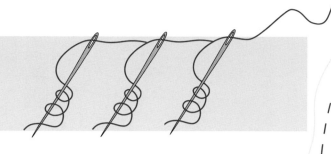

Appliqué Medallion

Approximate Size
34" x 34"

Appliqué Block Size
9" x 9" finished

Tip: *To protect the edges, the background squares are cut oversized and trimmed to the correct size just before stitching the quilt top together.*

Materials

Blocks
$^3/_8$ yard red (background, cornerstones, flowers)
$^3/_8$ yard violet (background, flowers)
$^3/_8$ yard blue-green (background, flowers)
$^1/_4$ yard black print for stems
Assorted scraps for accent colors
Clear plastic or mylar
$^1/_4$" bias bar
Finishing
$^1/_2$ yard black (sashing, finishing triangles)
$^1/_2$ yard black/white (border, binding)
$1^1/_4$ yards backing
40" x 40" batting

Patterns
Floral Blocks 1, 2, 3, 4, 5 (pages 83 to 87)
Sashing and Cornerstone (page 82)

The setting for these five original appliqué blocks is a bit unusual. The blocks appear to be joined only with the red corners but, they are actually sashed with the background fabric. This type of setting makes the blocks appear to be floating on the background. It is a difficult looking technique that is quite easy to do. The appliqué blocks include some reverse appliqué and a little embroidery just for fun.

Tips

Review Applique Quilts in the General Directions, pages 147 to 155, before beginning.

It's unlikely that you will complete one of these applique blocks in one sitting. To make these complicated designs more portable, baste the pieces to the background fabric after they have been prepared using Basic Freezer Paper Techniques, page 149.

Cutting

Note: *Make templates for Appliqué Shapes, Corner-stones and Sashing*

Blocks

2 squares, 12" x 12", red (background)
2 squares, 12" x 12", violet (background)
1 square, 12" x 12", blue-green (background)

Finishing

2 squares, 9½" x 9½", black, cut in half on the diagonal (corner triangles)
1 square, 14½" x 14½", black, cut in quarters on the diagonal (side triangles)
12 rectangles, 2" x 9½", black (sashing)
8 squares, 2" x 2", red (cornerstones)
4 strips, 2" x width of fabric, black/white (border)
4 strips, 2" x width of fabric, black/white (binding)

Instructions

Blocks

1. There are five appliqué blocks in this quilt with three different backgrounds. (**Diagram 1**) Read Appliqué, pages 147 to 155, before you begin.

Floral Block 1

Floral Block 2

Floral Block 3

Floral Block 4

Floral Block 5

Diagram 1

2. Make a cardboard template the size of the finished appliqué block, 9" x 9". Use this to mark the piecing line on the wrong side of each background square. (**Diagram 2**)

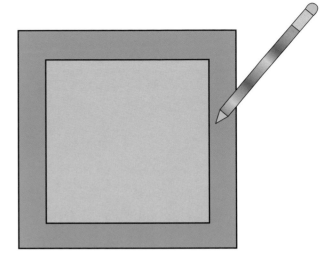

Diagram 2

3. Referring to Preparing the Background Fabric for Appliqué, page 152, make centering guidelines and prepare a transparent overlay for each block. These steps will assure that the elements of the design are laid out correctly.

4. Appliqué each of the five blocks. Use freezer paper for flowers and leaves. Use bias bars, referring to page 152, for stems. Trim the finished appliqué blocks to 9½" x 9½".

Note: *Mark inside of each sashing strip and corner-stone using the templates to create accurate stitching guidelines.*

Finishing

Note: *Read Finishing Up, pages 161 to 174, and complete your quilt.*

1. Lay out the sashing, cornerstones and the appliqué blocks. Pay attention to the direction in which you place the blocks. Two of the blocks are directional. (**Diagram 3**)

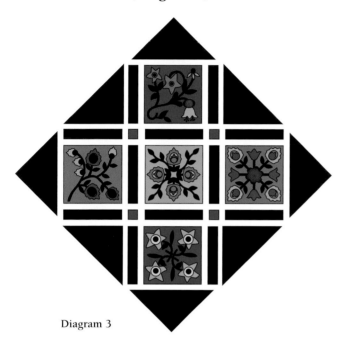

Diagram 3

2. Sew blocks, sashing and cornerstones together in rows as shown in **Diagram 4**.

Diagram 4

3. Sew the side triangles to the two block and sashing units. Finally sew the corner triangles to the corners. (**Diagram 5**) Press.

Diagram 5

4. Measure the sides of the quilt and cut four 2"-wide black/white border strips to this measurement. Sew one to the top and one to the bottom of the quilt. Next sew 2" red cornerstones to the ends of the two remaining borders and sew to the sides of the quilt. (**Diagram 6**)

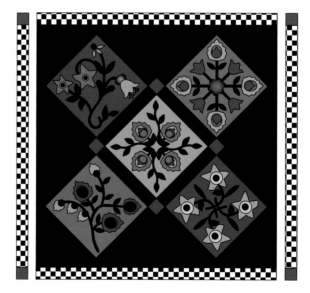

Diagram 6

5. Layer the quilt top, batting and backing together with the wrong sides of the quilt top and backing facing the batting. Baste or pin the layers together. Quilt or tie as desired.

6. Finish the edge of the quilt with continuous binding. Add a label to the quilt back.

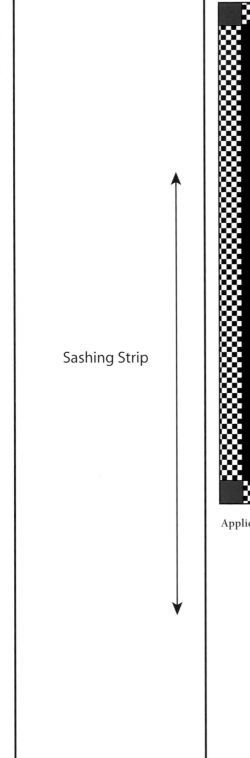

Sashing Strip

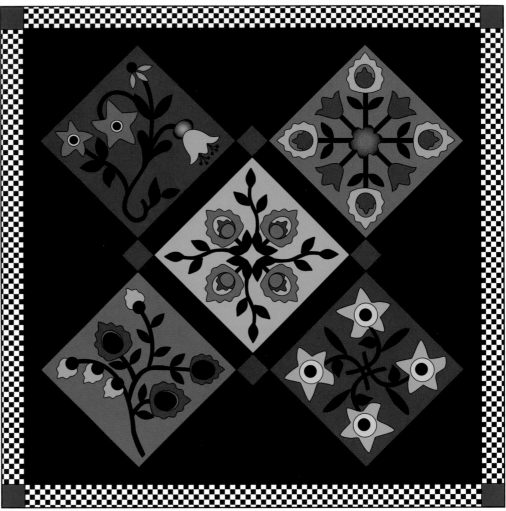

Appliqué Medallion Quilt Layout

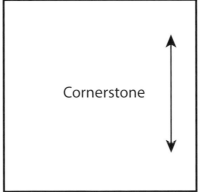

Cornerstone

Floral Block 1

Floral Block 2

Floral Block 4

Floral Block 5

Courthouse Steps Log Cabin

Approximate Size
63" x 73½"

Block Size
10½" x 10½" finished

Materials

Blocks
¼ yard, each, light print and dark print, for centers
6 yards various light scraps
6 yards various dark scraps
Template Material

Finishing
⅝ yard red (binding)
4 yards backing
67" x 77" batting

Patterns
Courthouse Steps A, B, C, D, E, F and G (page 93)

Cutting

Notes: *Make templates for A, B, C, D, E, F and G. Or, use rotary cutting tools or scissors to pre-cut strips. From these strips cut the squares and rectangles. After cutting the required squares and rectangles, mark inside each one using the templates to create accurate stitching guidelines. The measurements given below include the seam allowance.*

TIP: *Cut scraps into strips 1⅜" x length of scrap. Be sure to cut on the straight of the grain. Do not cut strips on the bias. Separate strips into light and dark stacks.*

The Courthouse Steps Log Cabin quilt pattern is complicated looking, but the blocks are easy to piece and to sew together. This particular style of Log Cabin quilt is made of two types of blocks set side by side in an alternating pattern. The piecing of each block is identical—the position of the colored strips is what makes the blocks different.

The Log Cabin style quilt is easy for beginning quiltmakers. This quilt type has so many variations that even very experienced quiltmakers continue to find them interesting and engaging to make.

The sizes of the long rectangles make this an ideal quilt style for many, many light and dark scraps. Ideally Log Cabin quilts are composed of highly contrasting values opposite each other for the signature dramatic look.

Template Tip

If the fabric moves too much while the templates are being traced, place a piece of fine-grain sandpaper under the fabric. The roughness of the sandpaper will make the fabric easier to mark.

Blocks

2 strips, $2^{1}/4$" x width of fabric, light print, cut into:
   21 A squares, $2^{1}/4$" x $2^{1}/4$"

2 strips, $2^{1}/4$" x width of fabric, dark print, cut into:
   21 A squares, $2^{1}/4$" x $2^{1}/4$"

3 strips, $1^{3}/8$" x width of fabric, light prints, cut into:
   42 B rectangles, $1^{3}/8$" x $2^{1}/4$"

3 strips, $1^{3}/8$" x width of fabric, dark prints, cut into:
   42 B rectangles, $1^{3}/8$" x $2^{1}/4$"

9 strips, $1^{3}/8$" x width of fabric, light prints, cut into:
   84 C rectangles, $1^{3}/8$" x 4"

9 strips, $1^{3}/8$"" x width of fabric, dark prints, cut
   into: 84 C rectangles, $1^{3}/8$" x 4"

13 strips, $1^{3}/8$" x width of fabric, light prints, cut
   into: 84 D rectangles, $1^{3}/8$" x $5^{3}/4$"

13 strips, $1^{3}/8$" x width of fabric, dark prints, cut
   into: 84 D rectangles, $1^{3}/8$" x $5^{3}/4$"

16 strips, $1^{3}/8$" x width of fabric, light prints, cut
   into: 84 E rectangles, $1^{3}/8$" x $7^{1}/2$"

16 strips, $1^{3}/8$" x width of fabric, dark prints, cut
   into: 84 E rectangles, $1^{3}/8$" x $7^{1}/2$"

20 strips, $1^{3}/8$" x width of fabric, light prints, cut
   into: 84 F rectangles, $1^{3}/8$" x $9^{1}/4$"

20 strips, $1^{3}/8$" x width of fabric, dark prints, cut
   into: 84 F rectangles, $1^{3}/8$" x $9^{1}/4$"

12 strips, $1^{3}/8$" x width of fabric, light prints, cut
   into: 42 G rectangles, $1^{3}/8$" x 11"

12 strips, $1^{3}/8$" x width of fabric, dark prints, cut
   into: 42 G rectangles, $1^{3}/8$" x 11"

Finishing

8 strips, $2^{1}/2$" x width of fabric, red (binding)

Instructions

Piecing the Blocks

1. There are two kinds of blocks in this quilt. Block
   A, has a dark center with dark outer logs. Block
   B has a light center with light outer logs.
   (**Diagram 1**)

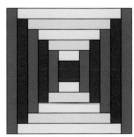

Block A   Block B

Diagram 1

2. Stitch two B Rectangles to the A Square. Alternate
   dark with light, light with dark. (**Diagram 2**)

Diagram 2

3. Continue piecing each block, adding Rectangles
   in alphabetical order. (**Diagrams 3 to 8**) Piece
   21 A blocks with dark centers and 21 B blocks
   with light centers.

Diagram 3

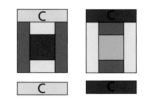

Diagram 4

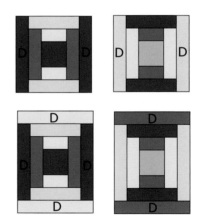

Diagram 5

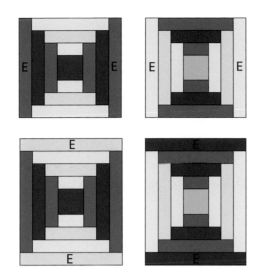

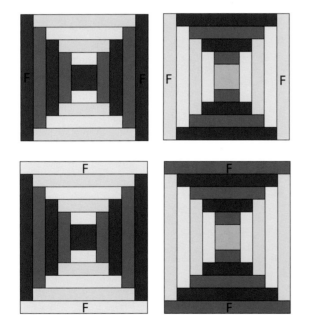

Diagram 6

Diagram 7

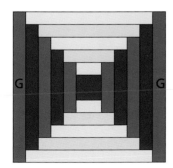

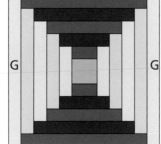

Diagram 8

Finishing the Quilt

Note: *Read Finishing Up, pages 161 to 174, and complete your quilt.*

1. Lay out the blocks into seven rows of six blocks each. Alternate light-centered blocks with the dark-centered blocks. (**Diagram 9**)

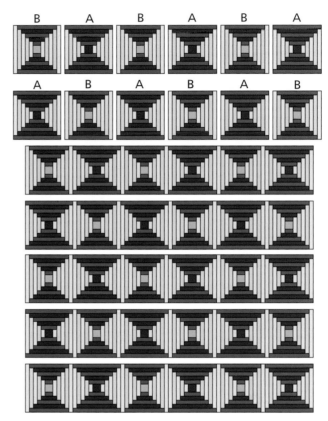

Diagram 9

2. Stitch the blocks together. Press and then stitch the rows together.

3. Layer the quilt top, batting and backing together with the wrong sides of the quilt top and backing facing the batting. Baste or pin the layers together. Quilt or tie as desired.

4. Finish the edge of the quilt with continuous binding. Add a label to the quilt back.

Courthouse Steps Quilt Layout

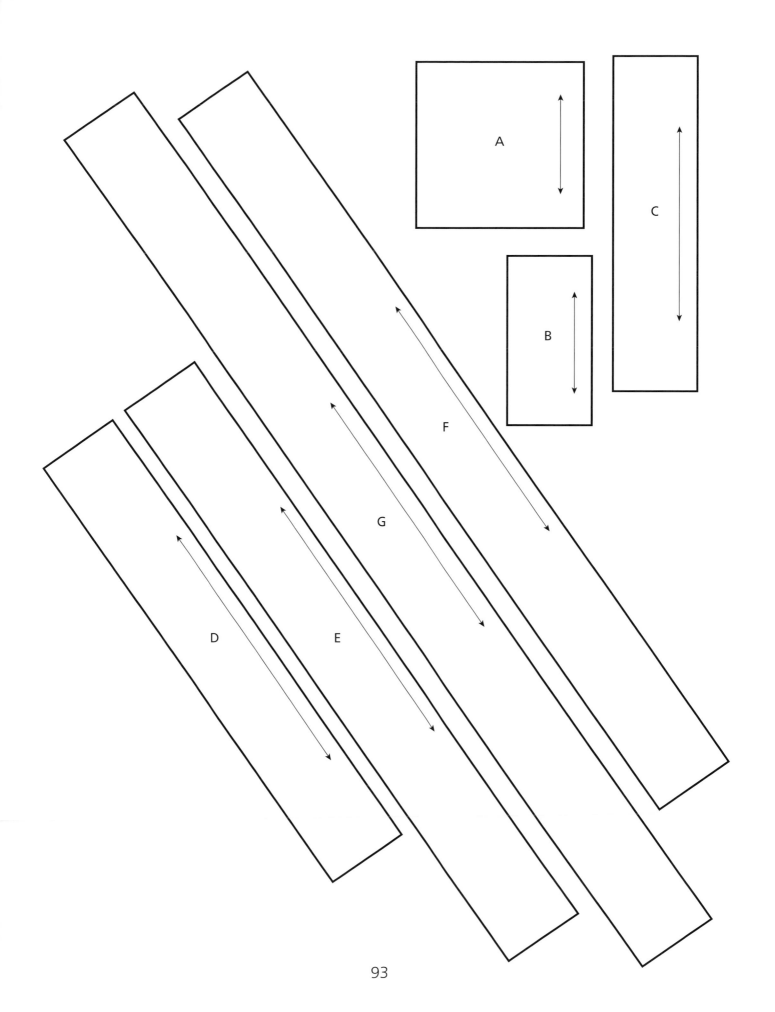

93

Indiana Puzzle

Approximate Size
64" x 76"

Block Size
6" x 6" finished

Notes: *Please read the General Directions, pages 142 to 174, before you begin. Fabric quantities specified are for 42" - 44" wide, 100% cotton fabrics. Templates* **do not** *include seam allowances. Strip-cut measurements* **do** *include seam allowances. Use a* $^1/4$" *seam allowance. Sew with right sides together. Press seams as you go.*

Materials
Blocks
$6^1/2$ yards red (includes border)
$6^1/4$ yards white (includes binding)
Template material

Finishing
4 yards backing
68" x 80" batting

Patterns
Indiana Puzzle A, B, C and D (page 99)

Cutting
Note: *Make plastic templates for A, B, C and D. Label the templates with all notations.*

Blocks
440 A, red
440 A, white
440 B, red
440 B, white
440 C, red
440 C, white
440 D, red
440 D, white

Finishing
7 strips, $2^1/2$"x width of fabric, red (border)
7 strips, $2^1/2$" x width of fabric, white (binding)

This is an old tessellating design. This particular variation has 220 blocks. Although the quilt is a family quilt from Indiana no one remembers who made it! There are a few clues to its maker. The patches are stitched by hand and machine and it is totally hand quilted. Maybe it was a group quilt. We'll never know.
The individual blocks are easy to assemble. To achieve the tessellating effect, a little care must be taken to arrange the identical blocks by alternating the larger red triangles up or down.

Instructions

Piecing the Block

1. Sew a red A Square to a white A Square; repeat. Sew pairs together to make a four patch. (**Diagram 1**)

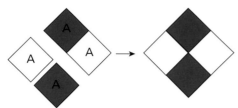

Diagram 1

Note: *All of the blocks should be pieced in the same way with the colors always in the same position.*

2. Sew red B Triangles to opposite sides of the four patch. Sew white B Triangles to remaining sides. (**Diagram 2**)

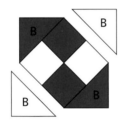

Diagram 2

3. Sew white C Triangles to opposite sides of the four patch. Sew red C Triangles to remaining sides. (**Diagram 3**)

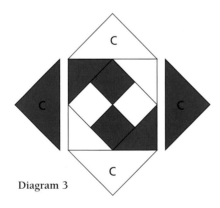

Diagram 3

4. Sew red D Triangles to opposite sides of the four patch. Sew white D Triangles to remaining sides. (**Diagram 4**)

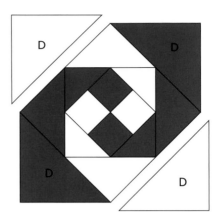

Diagram 4

5. Repeat steps 1 to 4 for the remaining 219 blocks in the quilt.

Tip: *Keep a finished block next to you as you complete all the blocks to remind you of the direction of the piecing.*

Finishing the Quilt

Note: *Read Finishing Up, pages 161 to 174, and complete your quilt.*

1. Lay out the quilt in twelve rows with ten blocks in each row. Alternate the direction of each block as you lay out the row. There are two kinds of rows: #1 and #2. (**Diagram 5**) All odd rows are #1 and all even rows are #2.

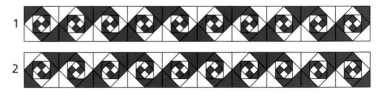

Diagram 5

Tip: *Since there are so many blocks in this quilt, it would be very easy to mix up the blocks or the rows. Stitch a row or two together; then hold the panel up to a mirror to see if there are any errors.*

2. Continue laying out the blocks and stitching the rows until you have completed the body of the quilt. (**Diagram 6**)

Diagram 6

3. Measure the quilt top and cut the $2^1/_2$"-wide red border strips to fit the sides of the quilt. Sew the side borders. Repeat for the top and bottom of the quilt. Sew these final borders in place.

4. Layer the quilt top, batting and backing together with the wrong sides of the quilt top and backing facing the batting. Baste or pin the layers together. The larger white and red areas are quilted with a square motif. The remainder of the quilting follows the pieces.

5. Finish the edge of the quilt with continuous binding. Add a label to the quilt back.

Indiana Puzzle Quilt Layout

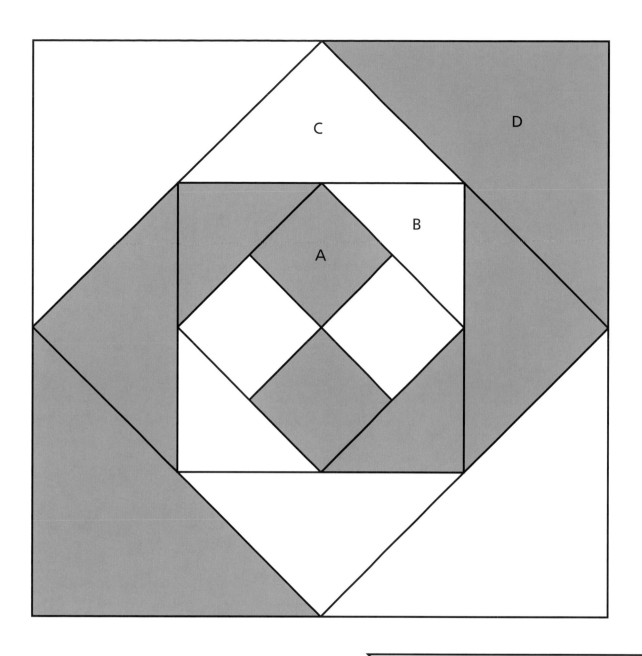

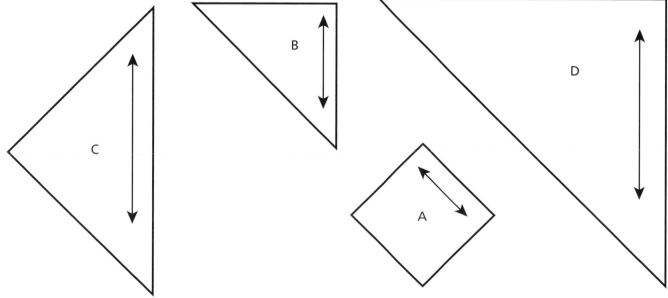

Whig Rose

Approximate Size
48" x 54"

Block Size
9" x 9" finished

Notes: *Please read the General Directions, pages 142 to 174, before you begin, especially The Stenciled Quilt, page 155. Fabric quantities specified are for 42" - 44" wide, 100% cotton fabrics. Templates **do not** include seam allowances. Strip-cut measurements **do** include seam allowances. Use a ¼" seam allowance. Sew with right sides together. Press seams as you go.*

Materials

Blocks
2½ yards muslin (includes pieced sawtooth border)
⅓ yard assorted red print scraps (pieced sawtooth border)
⅛ yard red print (appliqué flower centers)
Erasable fabric marker
Versatex™ fabric paint, pink, red, green, and blue
Freezer paper for stencil
Craft knife (or scissors)
2 Stencil brushes
1 skein black embroidery floss

Finishing
1 yard dark red print (outer border and binding)
3 yards backing
52" x 62" batting

Patterns
Whig Rose Block (page 107)
Appliqué Circle (page 107)
Whig Rose Flower Border (page 108)
Leaf Stencil (page 109)
Sawtooth Border Stencil (page 109)
Pieced Border Triangle (page 109)

This is a type of whole-cloth quilt similar to those made at the height of their fashion, c.1800 – 1840. This, however, is a contemporary quilt, completed in 2006, using modern fabric paints and fabrics to replicate an older style quilt. The colors are traditional. The whole cloth quilt is embellished with appliqué, embroidery and a patchwork outer border. The inner red sawtooth border is stenciled.

Cutting

Stenciled Quilt Center

1 rectangle, $40^1/2$" x $46^1/2$", muslin

Finishing

90 Border Triangles, muslin (pieced sawtooth border)

90 Border Triangles, red prints (pieced sawtooth border)

12 strips, $2^1/2$" x width of fabric, red print (outer border and binding)

Instructions

Stenciled Quilt Center

Note: *Read The Stenciled Quilt, pages 155 to 158, before beginning.*

1. Using the pre-washed and ironed muslin, mark guidelines for the blocks and the stenciled Sawtooth border. Use a very light touch and a removable marker. Take care to measure correctly. Make an 'X' across each of the twelve 9" x 9" blocks to facilitate centering the stencil design. (**Diagram 1**)

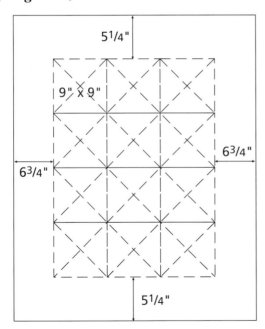

Diagram 1

Note: *The muslin measurements will allow the final patchwork border to fit correctly.*

2. Use one sheet of freezer paper, 2" or 3" larger than the Block for each of the three color separations. Trace each color grouping onto the dull side of the paper and cut out the design using a craft knife. The cut stencils are reusable if you use them carefully. Make two copies of each separation to finish the quilt. (**Diagram 2**)

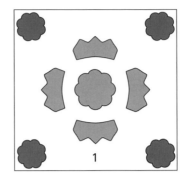
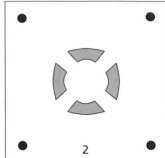
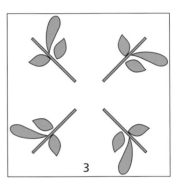

Diagram 2

Tip: *To save time, layer one or two additional sheets under the first sheet of freezer paper and cut all at the same time.*

Tip for Beginners: *Stencil #3 could be divided into two stencils - one with the stems and one with only the leaves.*

3. Center stencil #1 on one of the drawn 9" x 9" squares. Press the freezer paper onto the muslin with a warm iron. Make sure the design is well centered.

4. Stencil the corner flowers using a dry-brush technique and red paint; stencil the center flower and petals with pink paint. Carefully lift the stencil from the first block and set it aside to dry. Pick up the other #1 stencil and repeat the step for the next block. Complete all twelve blocks using stencil #1. Let dry completely.

Note: *Alternate the use of two identical stencils. By the time you have finished stenciling the second block the first stencil should be dry enough to use again.*

5. Stenciling the Accent Colors: Pick up stencil #2 and place over the first square and center on the previously stenciled area. Using the dry-brush technique and blue paint, lightly stencil the centers on the small flowers and the areas at the base of the four flower petals. The blue paint should give these areas a violet cast. Let dry completely. Repeat for all twelve squares.

6. Stenciling the Green: Pick up stencil #3 and place over the dry previously stenciled areas. Stencil the green being careful to lighten the stenciling where the stems meet the flowers. Let dry completely. Repeat these steps for all twelve squares. (**Diagram 3**)

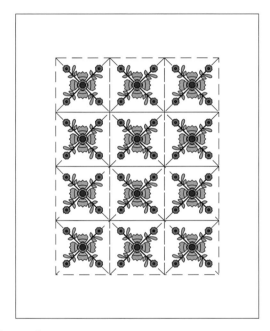

Diagram 3

7. Finish stenciling the body of the quilt by adding the four leaves at the corners of the 9" blocks as illustrated. (**Diagram 4**) Let dry completely. Press or heat-treat all the stenciling following the manufacturer's instructions.

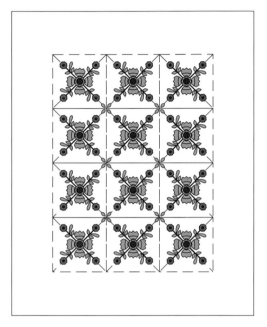

Diagram 4

8. Stenciled Sawtooth Border: Cut several Triangle Border stencils from freezer paper. Trace the triangles and mark the line on the papers. Cut out the triangles with a craft knife. (**Diagram 5**)

Diagram 5

9. Stencil the sawtooth border in sections. Paint three triangles red and then three more red triangles next to them. (**Diagram 6**)

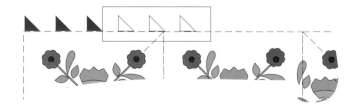

Diagram 6

103

10. Go back and fill in between the first three. (**Diagram 7**)

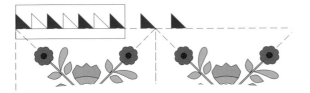

Diagram 7

11. Complete all four sides using this technique. Notice that there are NO TRIANGLES at the corners of the sides, top and bottom rows of the stenciled sawtooth border (**Diagram 8**) Let the stenciling dry completely and heat-set according to the manufacturers' directions.

Diagram 8

TIP: *If you are uncertain as to your ability to 'freehand' this border, you can measure and mark 27 one-inch squares at the top and bottom of the central panel and measure and mark 36 one-inch squares at each side of the central panel. Next stencil a triangle into each of these squares.*

Stenciled Floral Border

Note: *The remaining areas of the muslin will be covered with a free-flowing stenciled floral border. For this border, cut the stencils allowing for mirror images. Review Cutting Mirror Image Stencils, page 157, for creating mirrored images.*

1. Create three color-separated stencils for the border designs in same manner as for the Whig Rose Block in step 2 on page 102. Layer and cut two or three stencil layers at a time.

2. Begin by stenciling the corner elements first. Note that the stems and leaves are mirrored and turn at the central flower in the corner. Stencil the colors in the same order and using the same technique as for the Whig Rose Blocks. Join the two corner design elements (stems) at the notation, A, shown on the pattern (page 108).

3. Fill in the top, bottom and sides of the stenciled border using the two remaining design elements of a small flower swag and single Rose and stem. (**Diagram 9**) Let the stenciling dry completely and heat-set according to the manufacturer's directions.

Diagram 9

Tip: *Don't be afraid to be playful with these design elements. Create your own version of the stenciled border!*

Pieced Border

1. Piece together 94 red triangles and 94 muslin triangles to complete 94 half-square triangle units. Press seams to the red side. (**Diagram 10**)

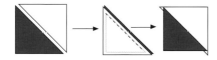

Diagram 10

2. Stitch together two strips of 20 half-square triangles to create the top and bottom border pieces. Stitch together two strips of 27 half-square triangles to create the sides of the pieced border.

3. Sew the top and bottom strips to the body of the quilt. Sew the sides to the body of the quilt.

4. Measure the quilt crosswise and cut two $2\frac{1}{2}$"-wide dark red strips to that length. Sew to top and bottom of quilt. Measure the quilt lengthwise and cut two $2\frac{1}{2}$"-wide to that length. Sew to sides of the quilt.

Embellishing the Stenciled Quilt

1. Cut 26 Appliqué Circles from freezer paper using pattern on page 108. Iron these paper circles to the red print fabric. Leave a scant $\frac{1}{2}$" between each circle. Cut Circles from the fabric including a scant $\frac{1}{4}$" seam allowance around each paper Circle.

2. Prepare Circles for appliqué referring to Perfect Circles, page 151, and stitch in place over the center of each larger flower in the blocks and the border. Using the black embroidery floss, sew a Blanket stitch around each large stenciled flower. (**Diagram 11**)

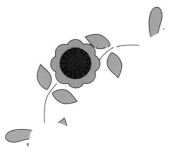

Diagram 11

Finishing the Quilt

Note: *Read Finishing Up, pages 161 to 174, and complete your quilt.*

1. Before layering the quilt, mark the background grid behind the Whig Rose Blocks by drawing lines with a erasable fabric marker joining the stenciled sawtooth triangles. The resulting squares are about $\frac{3}{4}$" x $\frac{3}{4}$". (**Diagram 12**)

Diagram 12

2. Layer the quilt top, batting and backing together with the wrong sides of the quilt top and backing facing the batting. Baste or pin the layers together. Quilt following the lines of the block, border designs and the gridlines.

3. Finish the edge of the quilt with continuous binding. Add a label to the quilt back.

Whig Rose Quilt Layout

Whig Rose Block Stencil Pattern

Applique
Circle

Whig Rose Flower Border Stencil Pattern

A

A

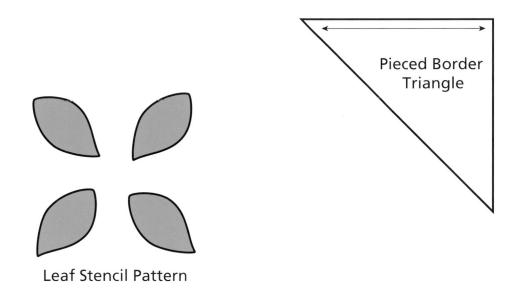

Pieced Border Triangle

Leaf Stencil Pattern

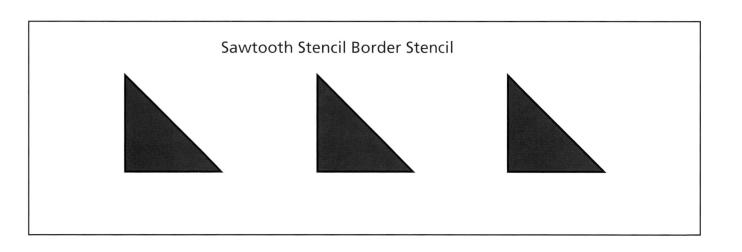

Sawtooth Stencil Border Stencil

The Music Lesson

Approximate Size
21³/₄" x 21³/₄"

Monkey Wrench Block Size
6" x 6"

Materials
Blocks
³/₄ yard muslin
¹/₄ yard red print
¹/₄ yard brown print (includes border)
1 skein Rosie Red embroidery floss
Embroidery needles
Embroidery hoop
Wash-out fabric marker

Finishing
¹/₄ yard red print (binding)
³/₄ yard backing
24" x 24" batting

Patterns
Monkey Wrench Block A, B (page 114)
The Music Lesson Embroidery Design (page 115)

Cutting
Block
1 square, 10" x 10", muslin (embroidery)
16 A, red print (Monkey Wrench block)
20 B, red print (Monkey Wrench block)
16 A, brown print (Monkey Wrench block)
16 B, brown print (Monkey Wrench block)

Finishing
4 rectangles, 6¹/₂" x 10", brown print (border)
3 strips, 2¹/₂" x width of fabric, red print (binding)

In the heart of every quiltmaker is the desire to collect old quilts, quilting tools, and even fragments of quilts and needlework. The Music Lesson quilt is the result of such a quest. Notice that the design of the Monkey Wrench blocks is very similar to that of those in the Shoo-Fly quilt, page 122. The actual drafting of the design is different and based on a different block system.

The Music Lesson quilt is constructed from four antique Monkey Wrench blocks found in a thrift shop. Five blocks were found, in excellent condition, and the best of the five were used in this quilt. The embroidery design in the center of the quilt was probably made by a child at the end of the nineteenth century when Redwork was a popular embroidery style. The design was not centered on the background fabric—drifting off the edge of the fabric—and maybe not completed. I redrew the design onto a new background fabric and embroidered it close in technique to the original.

Instructions

Embroidered Center

1. Center the 10" muslin square over the Music Lesson design from page 115. Using a wash-out fabric marker, trace the design onto the fabric.

2. Thread an embroidery needle with about an 18" length of three strands of embroidery floss. Put the muslin in a small embroidery hoop to prepare it for the needlework.

3. Using the Blanket stitch, Stem stitch and French knots, complete The Music Lesson embroidery design. (**Diagram 1**)

Diagram 1

Blanket Stitch

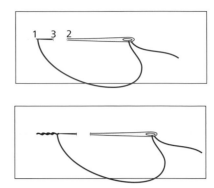

Stem Stitch

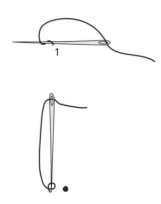

French Knot

Monkey Wrench Blocks

1. Sew a red print A Triangle and a brown print A Triangle together. (**Diagram 2**) Repeat for remaining A Triangles.

Diagram 2

2. Sew a red print B Square and a brown print B Square together. (**Diagram 3**) Repeat for 15 more pairs of B squares.

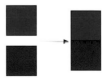

Diagram 3

3. Arrange four A units, four B units and a red print B Square to form a Monkey Wrench block. Sew units together in rows, then sew rows together to complete block. (**Diagram 4**) Make three more Monkey Wrench blocks.

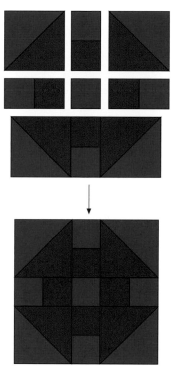

Diagram 4

Finishing the Quilt

Note: *Read Finishing Up, pages 161 to 174, and complete your quilt.*

1. Sew a 6^1/$_2$" x 10" brown print rectangle to top and bottom of embroidered center. (**Diagram 5**)

Diagram 5

2. Sew a Monkey Wrench block to each end of remaining 6^1/$_2$" x 10" rectangles. Sew to sides of embroidered center. (**Diagram 6**)

Diagram 6

3. Layer the quilt top, batting and backing together with wrong sides of quilt top and backing facing the batting. Baste or pin the layers together. Quilt or tie as desired.

4. Finish the edge of the quilt with continuous binding. Add a label to the quilt back.

113

The Music Lesson Quilt Layout

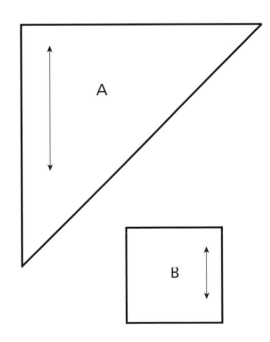

Cat and Bird
Embroidery Pattern

Provincial Stars

Approximate Size
20" x 24"

Star Block Size
4" x 4" finished

Materials

Blocks
8 fat eights (9" x 11") or scraps of light and medium prints

Finishing
$1/4$ yard red print (border)
$1/4$ yard yellow print (binding)
24" x 28" batting and backing

Note: *Extra binding and border fabric can be used in the body of the quilt.*

Patterns
Provincial Star patterns (page 121)
Heart Quilting Designs (page 121)

Note: *Make templates for the pieced star and label A, B, C, and D. Templates do not include seam allowances. Mark around each template on the wrong side of the fabrics. Remember to allow about $1/2$" around each tracing to allow for the seam allowance. Cut each piece from the fabric with a $1/4$" seam allowance.*

Cutting

Each Star Block
4 A, light or medium prints (background)
4 C, light or medium prints (background)
8 B, light or medium prints (star)
1 D, light or medium prints (star)

Finishing
2 rectangles, $4^1/2$" x $12^1/2$", red print (border)
2 rectangles, $4^1/2$" x $16^1/2$", red print (border)
3 strips, $2^1/4$" x width of fabric, yellow print (binding)

Doll and wall quilts are highly collectable. This version of a four-patch eight-pointed star is easy to piece and the quilt setting is uncomplicated. The sixteen blocks can go together in just a few remnants of time. The quilt is the perfect size for an 18-inch doll.

DESIGN TIP: *Repetition of Fabrics in Quilts*
One of the ways to help create a feeling of unity and harmony in a quilt design is to have each fabric repeated at least two times – in different parts of the design. This repetition creates both interest and movement in the quilt. Look at the photograph of the Provincial Stars quilt. Think about how the fabrics are used and placed.

Instructions

Making the Star Blocks

1. Separate the B and D pieces into one pile and the A and C pieces into a second pile. Coordinate background A and C pieces with pleasing Star B and D pieces to make blocks. (**Diagram 1**)

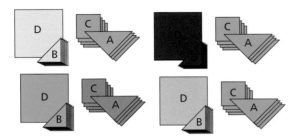

Diagram 1

2. Working with one block at a time, sew two B Triangles to an A Triangle. (**Diagram 2**) Repeat three more times.

Diagram 2

3. Sew an A/B unit to opposite sides of a D Square. (**Diagram 3**)

Diagram 3

4. Sew a C square to opposite sides of A/B. Repeat. Sew rows together to complete Star block. (**Diagram 4**) Repeat for 15 more Star blocks.

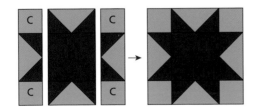

Diagram 4

Finishing the Quilt

Note: *Read Finishing Up, pages 161 to 174 to complete your quilt.*

1. Place Star blocks in four rows of three blocks each. Sew blocks together in rows then sew rows together. (**Diagram 5**) The remaining four blocks will be used in the border as cornerstones.

Diagram 5

2. Sew the $4^{1/2}$" x $12^{1/2}$" red print rectangles to the top and bottom of the quilt. Sew a Star block to opposite ends of a $4^{1/2}$" x $16^{1/2}$" red print rectangle; repeat. Sew to sides of quilt. (**Diagram 6**)

Diagram 6

3. Mark the Heart Quilting Design in the red print borders. Layer the quilt top, batting and backing together with the wrong sides of the quilt top and backing facing the batting. Baste or pin the layers together. Hand quilt.

4. Finish the edge of the quilt with continuous binding. Add a label to the quilt back.

Provincial Stars Quilt Layout

Provincial Star Patterns

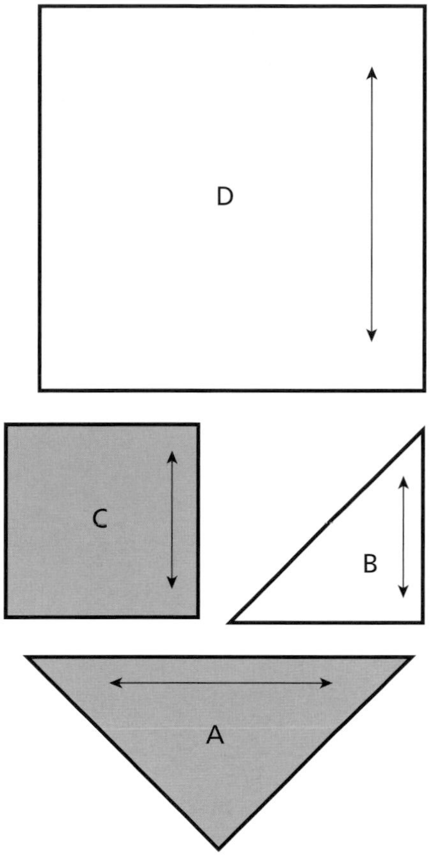

D

C

B

A

Full-size Placement Diagram

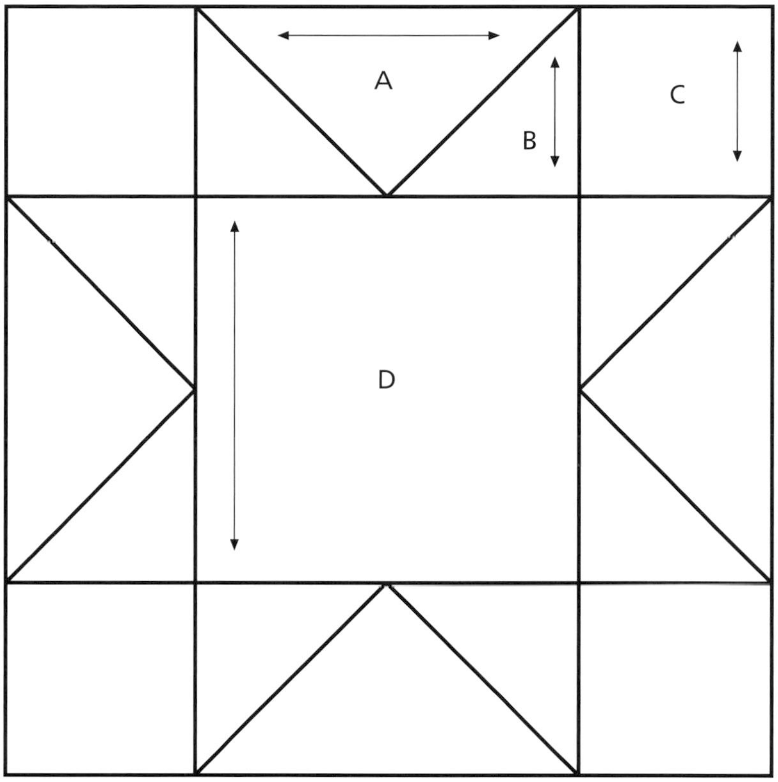

A

B

C

D

Heart Quilting Designs

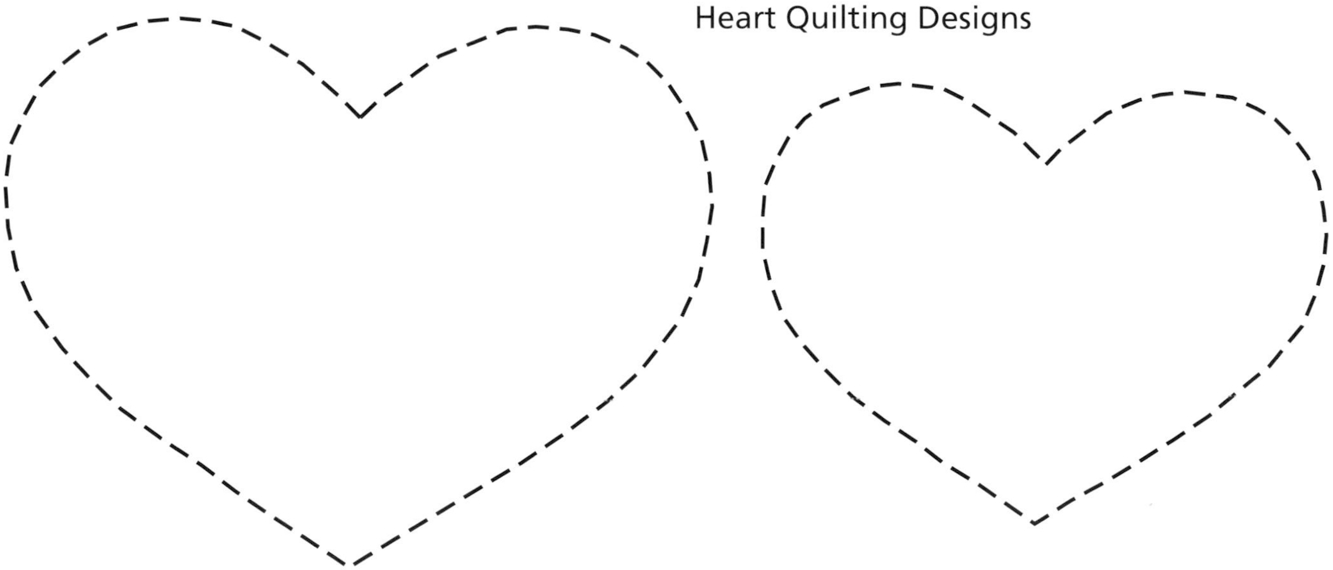

Shoo-fly

Approximate Size
20" x 24"

Block Size
3" x 3" finished

Notes: *Please read the General Directions, pages 142 to 174, before you begin. Fabric quantities specified are for 42" - 44" wide, 100% cotton fabrics. Templates* **do not** *include seam allowances. Strip-cut measurements* **do** *include seam allowances. Sew with right sides together. Press seams as you go.*

Materials

Blocks

$1/8$ yard dark brown (A and B)
$1/8$ yard light tan (A, B and C)
$1/4$ yard light background fabric (D, E and F)
$1/8$ yard medium tan or 12 scrap squares, 3?" x 3?" (Oak Leaves)

Finishing

$1/8$ yard taupe print (first border)
$1/3$ yard medium tan (second border and binding)
24" x 28" backing and batting
Fray-Check™ or other raw-edge treatment
1 skein black embroidery floss

Patterns

Shoo-fly Block A, B and C (page 127)
D Square (page 127)
E, F Triangle (page 127)
G Oak Leaf Appliqué (page 127)

The "Shoo-Fly" block is in the Nine-Patch family and it is a favorite among traditional quiltmakers. The doll quilt design contains twelve Shoo-Fly blocks set on point with six plain blocks in between the pieced blocks. The edges are finished with triangles. There is a narrow first border and a wider second border embellished with appliquéd Oak Leaves in each corner. The oak leaf is one I collected in the northern mountains of Arizona. You might want to substitute a wonderful leaf shape or other design that you have collected.

The sample quilt is made of scrap fabrics. The fabric amounts, given in the Materials list are for purchased fabric.

Cutting

Shoo-fly Blocks

Notes: *Trace and cut pieces according to the instructions. The cutting instructions are for all 12 of the Shoo-fly blocks.*

48 A, light tan
48 A, dark brown
48 B, light tan
48 B, dark brown
12 C, light tan

Finishing

6 D Squares, light background
10 E Triangles, light background
4 F Triangles, light background
2 strips, 1½" x width of fabric, taupe (first border)
3 strips, 3½" x width of fabric, medium tan (second border)
3 strips, 2½" x width of fabric, medium tan (binding)

Instructions

Making the Shoo-fly Blocks

1. Make templates A, B, C, D, E, F and G referring to page 127.

2. Trace around templates A, B, and C onto the light tan and dark brown fabrics. Mark the corners and points clearly and be sure to leave room for seam allowance. You will need 48 A, 48 B and 12 C from light tan and 48 A and 48 B from dark brown.

3. Cut pieces leaving about a ¼" seam allowance around each side.

4. Lay out all the pieces for one block.

HINT: *Lay out the pieces on a piece of scrap batting or flannel and pin them down to keep the pieces from shifting. This hint is especially important if you aren't able to finishing sewing the block in one sitting.*

5. Sew a light tan A Triangle and a dark brown A Triangle together. (**Diagram 1**) Make three more pieced squares.

Diagram 1

6. Sew light tan B and dark brown B together. (**Diagram 2**) Make three more pieced squares.

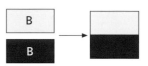

Diagram 2

7. Lay out the stitched pieces from steps 5 and 6 plus the light tan C Square. (**Diagram 3**)

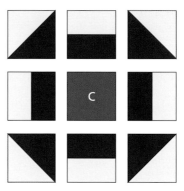

Diagram 3

8. Sew squares in rows then sew rows together. (**Diagram 4**)

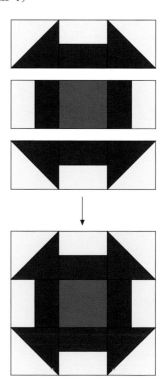

Diagram 4

9. On the light background fabric, trace around templates D, E, and F. Mark the points clearly and pay close attention to the grainline notations on the templates. You will need 6 D Squares, 10 E Triangles, and 4 F Triangles. Cut out pieces leaving a $^1/_4$" seam allowance around each side.

Finishing the Quilt

Note: *Read Finishing Up, pages 161 to 174, to complete your quilt.*

1. Lay out the Shoo-fly blocks, D squares, E triangles and F triangles in diagonal rows. (**Diagram 5**)

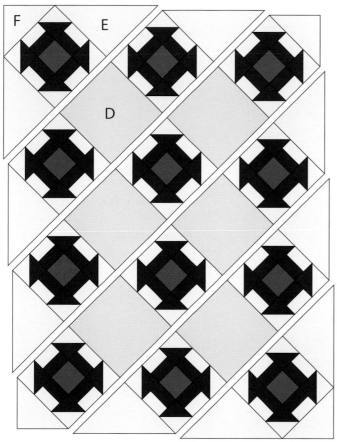

Diagram 5

2. Carefully pin and piece the body of the quilt together in diagonal strips. Assemble the strips to complete.

3. Measure quilt crosswise. Cut two $1^1/_2$"-wide taupe strips to that length. Attach the borders to the top and bottom of the quilt. Measure quilt lengthwise. Cut two $1^1/_2$"-wide taupe strips to that length. Sew to sides of quilt. Repeat for second border with $3^1/_2$"-wide medium tan strips.

4. Trace template G onto wrong side of medium tan fabric to create the Oak leaves. Before cutting the leaf shapes trace along each shape with Fray-Check™ (or diluted white glue). Let dry. Cut out each leaf along the traced line.

5. Referring to the quilt layout on page 126, pin the fabric leaves into place. Using two strands of black floss and a close Blanket stitch, attach each leaf to the quilt. (**Diagram 6**)

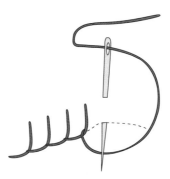

Diagram 6

6. Layer the quilt top, batting and backing together with the wrong sides of the quilt top and backing facing the batting. Baste or pin the layers together. Quilt as desired.

7. Finish the edge of the quilt with continuous binding. Add a label to the quilt back.

Shoo-fly Quilt Layout

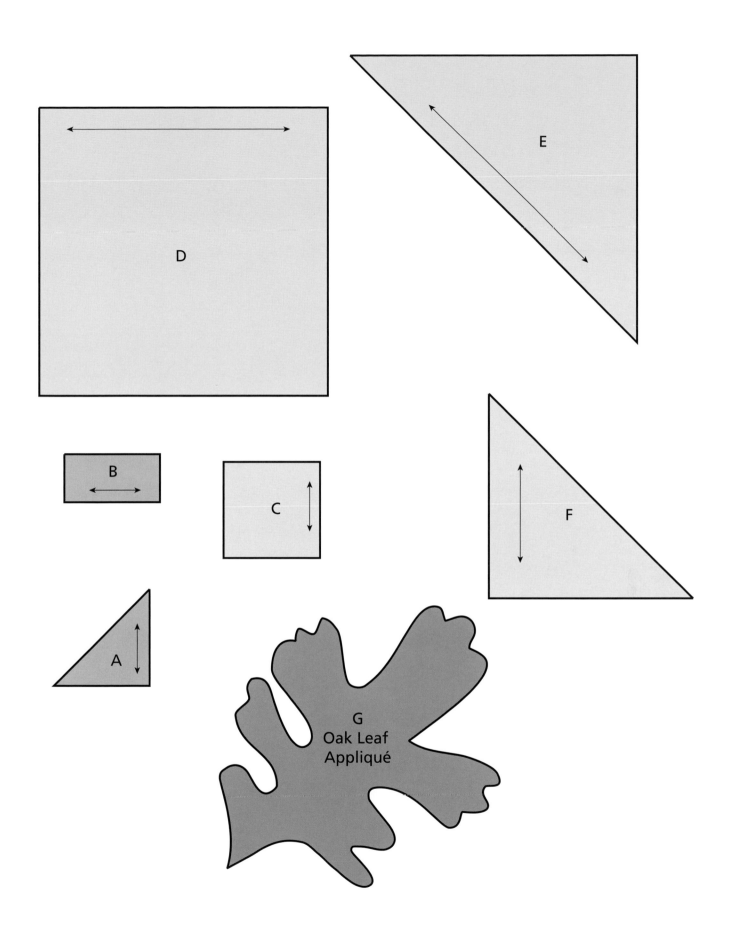

D

E

B

C

F

A

G
Oak Leaf
Appliqué

Summertime

Approximate Size
13½" x 13½"

Block Size
8" x 8" finished

Notes: *Please read the General Directions, pages 142 to 174, before you begin, especially The Stenciled Quilt, pages 155 to 158, and Appliqué Quilts, pages 147 to 155. Fabric quantities specified are for 42" - 44" wide, 100% cotton fabrics. Templates* **do not** *include seam allowances. Strip-cut measurements* **do** *include seam allowances. Use a ¼" seam allowance. Sew with right sides together. Press seams as you go.*

Materials

Block
1 fat quarter light background print
⅛ yard yellow print
8" square blue print
Various scraps for appliqué, blue, red, gold, and green
Versatex™ fabric paint, yellow, orange, and gold
Stencil brush
Freezer paper and craft knife or scissors
1 skein each embroidery floss, black and green
Matching thread (for appliqué)

Finishing
½ yard red check for binding and backing
15" x 15" square batting
Fat quarter backing fabric

Nice to Have: *Fine-grained sandpaper, plastic sheet protector, and permanent marker*

Patterns
Watering Can Appliqué (page 133)
Flower Motif Appliqué (page 134)
Flower with Bow Appliqué (page 135)

This happy little quilt is a perfect project for taking to the beach or a long trip. When finished it makes an ideal accent for a summer home or cottage. There is a little bit of everything to do – from piecing to appliqué – to stenciling and embroidery.

Cutting

1 square, $8^1/2$" x $8^1/2$", light background print
4 rectangles, 3" x $8^1/2$", yellow print (includes seam allowances)
4 squares, 3" x 3", blue print (includes seam allowance)

Instructions

Stenciling the Block

Note: *Read The Stenciled Quilt, pages 155 to 158, before beginning.*

1. Cut three freezer paper squares $8^1/2$" x $8^1/2$". Fold each square in quarters along the diagonal from corner to corner. These lines will help in centering the design on the fabric for stenciling. (**Diagram 1**)

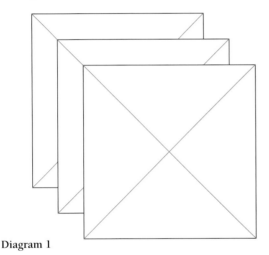

Diagram 1

2. Trace the parts of the watering can onto the three paper squares. Cut the freezer paper stencils for the watering can. (**Diagram 2**)

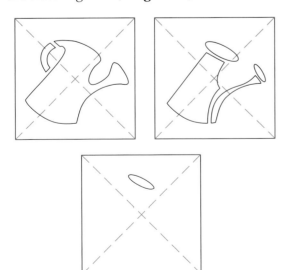

Diagram 2

3. Referring to The Stenciled Quilt, pages 155 to 158, stencil the watering can design onto the $8^1/2$" x $8^1/2$" light background square. Use a dry-brush technique and stencil lightly. Use the folds and the edges of the fabric and paper to aid in registration. Heat set the paint according to the manufacturer's directions. (**Diagram 3**)

Diagram 3

Tip: *Place a piece of fine-grained sandpaper under the fabric to keep it from shifting while stenciling.*

Sashing and Corner Squares

1. Mark the $^1/4$" seam lines on the wrong side of 3" x $8^1/2$" yellow print sashing rectangles and 3" x 3" blue print squares.

2. Stitch the top and bottom sashing rectangles to the stenciled square. Attach the corner squares to the remaining two sashing pieces and stitch to the sides of the quilt block. (**Diagram 4**)

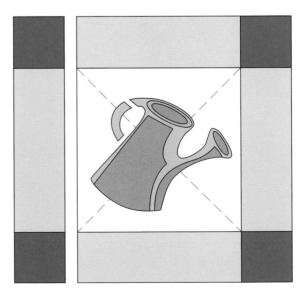

Diagram 4

Appliqué and Embroidery

1. Prepare the appliqué pieces using the Freezer Paper Technique, pages 149 to 150 with patterns on pages 133 to 135.

Tip: *Notice how the lower pieces of the ribbon appear to go around the handle of the watering can? Cut the freezer paper and fabric a little longer than on the worksheet. This step will make it easier for you to position the ribbon correctly on the handle and overlap it onto the sashing.*

2. Trace the appliqué motifs (pages 133 to 135) onto a plastic sheet protector to help in positioning the appliqué.

3. Position the appliqué pieces under the plastic sheet and pin in place. Remove the plastic and baste the pieces down to make the quilt more portable.

4. Appliqué the pieces in place using threads matching the pieces to appliquéd. (**Diagram 5**)

Diagram 5

Tip: *The beauty of appliqué is that the designs are artistic…they don't need to perfectly match the example. If a leaf slips a bit out of position, it will be just fine.*

5. Embroider the finishing touches on the quilt top. Outline the bow using the Backstitch and one strand of black embroidery floss. Embroider stamens on tulips using the Backstitch and French Knots with two strands of black floss. Outline the centers of red flowers with the Blanket stitch and two strands of black floss. Finally, make vines using the Backstitch and two strands of green embroidery floss.

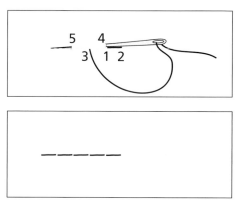

Backstitch

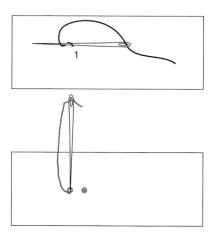

French Knot

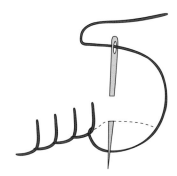

Blanket Stitch

131

Finishing the Quilt

Note: *Read Finishing Up, pages 161 to 174, to complete your quilt.*

1. Layer the quilt top, batting and backing together with the wrong sides of the quilt top and backing facing the batting. Baste or pin in place. Quilt as desired. Black quilting thread was used on the sample quilt. After quilting trim the edges of the batting and backing even with quilt top.

2. Hanging Triangles are perfect hanging devises for small quilts. See page 173, for details. Cut two 5" x 5" squares from backing fabric. Fold the squares in half on the diagonal with wrong sides together. Place at the top corners of the quilt on the back and pin in place.

3. Finish the edge of the quilt with continuous binding. **Note:** *The photographed quilt uses bias binding since a check fabric was used. See Bias-cut Mitered Binding, page 172.*

4. Add a label to the quilt back.

Summertime Quilt Layout

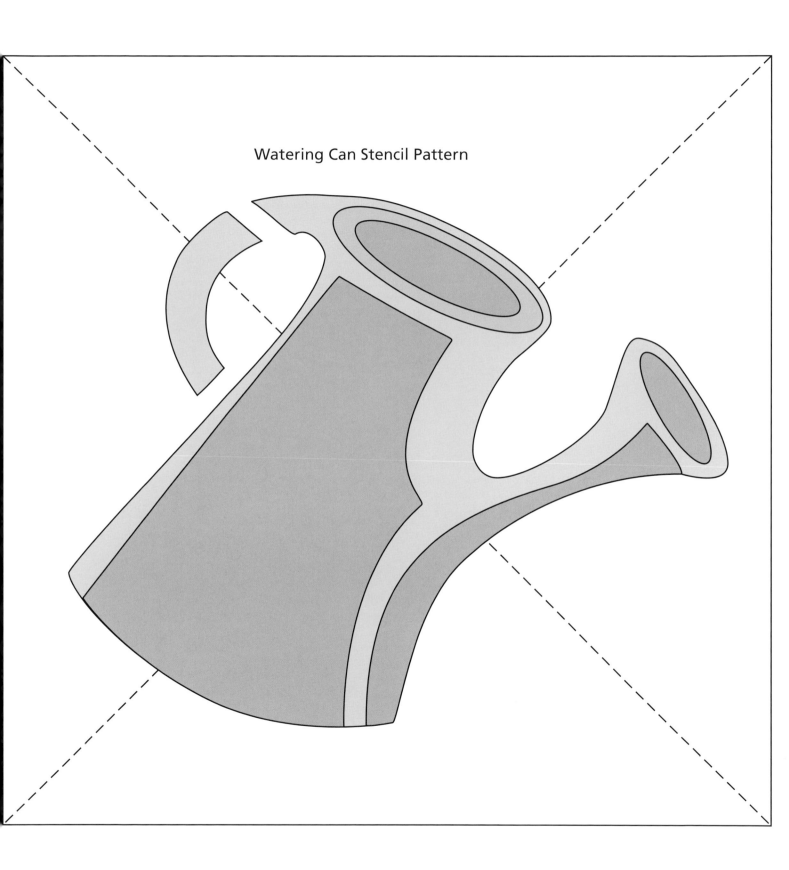

Watering Can Stencil Pattern

Flower Motif
Appliqué Pattern

Flower With Bow
Appliqué Pattern

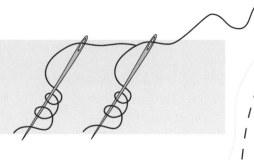

Evening Star

Approximate Size
45" x 45"

Star Block Size
29" x 29" finished

Notes: *Please read the General Directions, pages 142 to 174, before you begin. Fabric quantities specified are for 42" - 44" wide, 100% cotton fabrics. Template **does not** include seam allowances. Strip-cut measurements **do** include seam allowances. Use a ¹/4" seam allowance. Sew with right sides together. Press seams as you go.*

Materials
Star Block
¹/4 yard white print
¹/2 yard brown
¹/2 yard black print
1 yard muted plaid (background, first border)
Template material

Finishing
¹/4 yard blue (second border)
²/3 yard dark print (third border)
¹/3 yard dark plaid (binding)
2 yards backing
49" x 49" batting

Pattern
Evening Star Diamond (page 140)

Cutting
Note: *Make template for Diamond.*

Star Block
16 Diamonds, white print
32 Diamonds, brown
24 Diamonds, black print
4 squares, 8¹/2" x 8¹/2", muted plaid
1 square, 12¹/2" x 12¹/2", muted plaid (cut in quarters on the diagonal for side triangles)

The multifaceted star design, like this one, has had many names in the history of quiltmaking - Star of Bethlehem, Prairie Star, Lone Star, and Evening Star - to name a few. The colors in these stars radiate from the center and appear to pulse with an inner light.
This Evening Star Quilt is small in scale and simple in construction. Each of the eight points of the star is a diamond-shaped nine-patch block.

Design Tip

One of the greatest joys of being a quiltmaker is seeing more possibilities in a quilt designed by another. Choosing a pattern and fabrics, and finishing a quilt that one has altered - even slightly - from the original, gives most quiltmakers added pleasure.

As an added bonus you will find, on page 141, an alternate design for the hand quilted squares in the Evening Star Quilt. The fabrics chosen for the sample quilt have a somewhat contemporary look to them. If you choose more traditional fabrics you could hand quilt the Feathered Wreath in the squares.

Finishing

4 strips, $2^{1}/_{2}$" x width, muted plaid (first border)

4 strips, 2" x width, blue (second border)

5 strips, $4^{1}/_{2}$" x width of fabric, dark print (third border)

5 strips, $2^{1}/_{2}$" x width of fabric, dark plaid (binding)

Instructions

Making the Center

1. Lay out the first set of Diamonds into the shape of one point of the Evening Star. It will look like a diamond-shaped nine-patch block. (**Diagram 1**)

Diagram 1

2. Place two Diamonds right sides together and push a pin through the seam allowances at each end of the piecing line; sew seam. (**Diagram 2**)

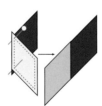

Diagram 2

3. Sew remaining Diamond to form a strip. (**Diagram 3**) Sew remaining two rows of Diamonds.

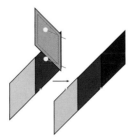

Diagram 3

4. Pin the first two strips together matching the corner seam lines for accurate joining of the strips. (**Diagram 4**)

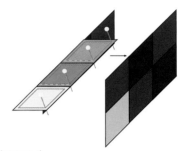

Diagram 4

5. Sew remaining strip to strips sewn in step 4 to complete a star point. (**Diagram 5**) Repeat seven more times.

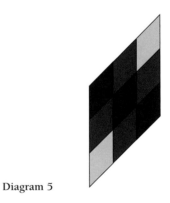

Diagram 5

6. Sew star points together in pairs. (**Diagram 6**)

Diagram 6

7. Sew one side of the large 8½" background square to the side of one star point. (**Diagram 7**)

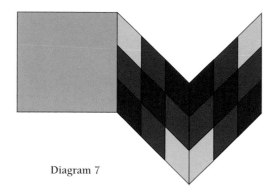

Diagram 7

8. Complete this section by insetting the background triangle between the star points. First sew one side of the triangle, then pivot the second side and continue stitching. (**Diagram 8**)

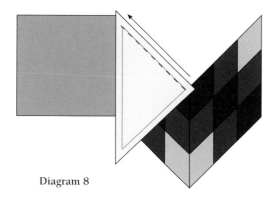

Diagram 8

9. After completing the quarter sections of the Evening Star, stitch them together from the center points toward the outer edge, pivoting where the star points join the corner squares. (**Diagram 9**)

Diagram 9

Finishing the Quilt

Note: *Read Finishing Up, pages 161 to 174, to complete your quilt.*

1. Measure quilt top lengthwise. Cut two 2½"-wide background strips to that length. Sew to sides of quilt. Measure the quilt top crosswise. Cut two 2½"-wide background strips to that length. Sew to top and bottom of quilt. **Note:** *The first border for the Evening Star is called a resting strip or floating strip because the same background fabric is used. The extra background strips make the star appear to float on the background.*

2. Attach the second and third borders in the same manner.

3. Layer the quilt top, batting and backing together with the wrong sides of the quilt top and backing facing the batting. Baste or pin layers together. Quilt as desired. Black quilting thread was used on the sample quilt. After quilting, trim the edges of the quilt even.

4. Finish the edge of the quilt with continuous binding. Add a label to quilt back.

Evening Star Quilt Layout

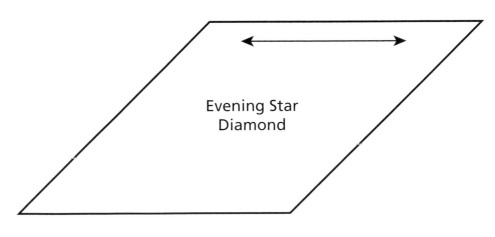

Evening Star
Diamond

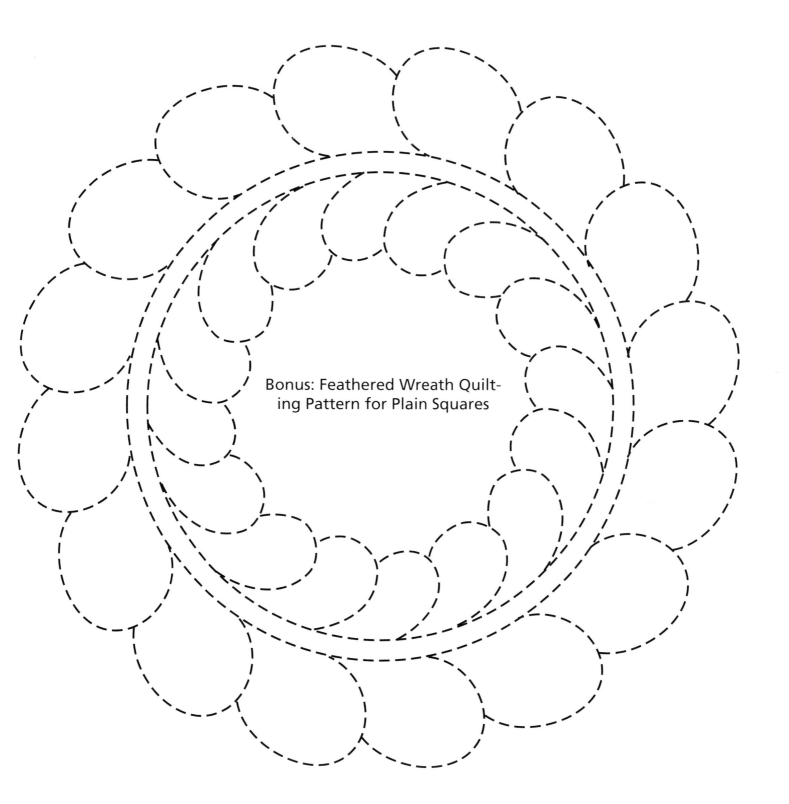

Bonus: Feathered Wreath Quilting Pattern for Plain Squares

Making a Quilt by Hand

Creating Your First Quilt

Unlike making a good apple pie, there is no precise recipe for making the perfect or ideal quilt. The quilt directions in this book will explain how to combine the elements within a particular quilt design. What you assemble for your fabrics and colors will be the special spice you bring to the quilt.

Each of the quilt designs in this book is made or presented to emphasize a certain technique or as an example to follow in planning your own quilts in the future. Each quilt presents a harmonious effect that is unified and agreeable.

Harmony means a pleasing arrangement. It's not always easy to achieve this effect. Practice and looking at good quilts will help you do it. The art of the quilt depends on the same elements of design found in other art:

Proportion - the association of one part of the design to another. The ratio of one size to another.

Balance - creating a sense of equilibrium in color, values, lines, space, and textures.

Rhythm - facilitating the movement of the eye from one part of the design to another in a fluid motion.

Emphasis - the dominance and accentuation of certain design elements like color, contrast/value, space, line, and texture.

Unity - coherence in the quilt design. All parts have the sense of belonging together. All parts relate to the design. Everything is complete.

"Every part is disposed to unity with the whole, that it may thereby escape its own incompleteness."

Leonardo da Vinci

Quilt Styles

Quiltmakers and historians continually uncover new clues into the history and techniques of this fascinating art. Every quilt, quilt style, quilt block, and even the colors used in a quilt offer up clues and tell a story if the viewer takes a moment to reflect on what is seen.

The following list mentions three of the most common quilt styles. Be aware that both older traditional, contemporary, and modern quilts often combine several design or style types to create a host of complex categories.

Whole cloth quilts are made from joining two pieces of fabric by tying or quilting them together.

Bar quilts, also called "strippies," are constructed of a few elongated rectangles occupying the body of the quilt. (**Diagram 1**)

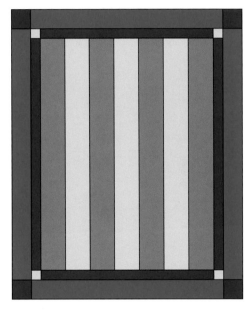

Diagram 1

One-patch quilts use specific geometric shapes that are stitched together in simple or complex patterns. (**Diagram 2**)

Diagram 2

The geometric shapes in patchwork have captured the imaginations of the contemporary quilter as much as they did in the nineteenth and twentieth centuries. The most common shape is a square. A square can be repeated in endless variety by changing fabrics and colors. There are other single shapes used in these one-patch quilts: triangle, hexagon, diamond, clamshell, rhomboid, gothic, and coffin. (**Diagram 3**)

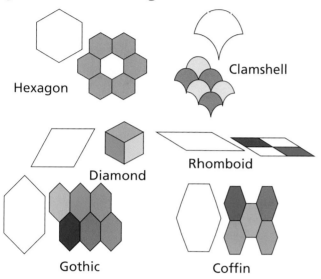

Diagram 3

Basic Grid Categories

The secret of learning to identify quilt block designs is to understand the system grid that is used to create the block design. Grids are made up of specific numbers of units.

Four-Patch: The four-patch is most often seen divided into 16 patches. It is still called a four-patch.

Nine-Patch: The nine-patch may be the most common of the grids. Don't be fooled by the simplicity of the nine squares—they can be made to design complex patterns—and they can be further divided into 36 squares!

Five-Patch: This is a grid system in which the block is divided into equal 25 squares. It is still called a five-patch.

Seven-Patch: This complex grid is divided into 49 squares, 7 x 7. It is called a seven-patch.

The final system of quilt design is not based on an equal grid system—it is divided by **Spokes**.

From these spokes come kaleidoscope designs, true eight-pointed stars, fans, and plates. (**Diagram 4**)

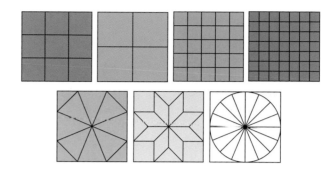

Diagram 4

Color and Fabric

Color

Although color attracts the eye and sets the mood of the quilt, it is the contrast between the colors used or the lights and darks in the quilt that defines the quilt pattern. (**Diagram 5**)

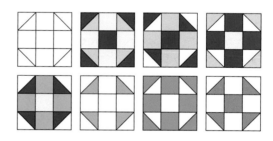

Diagram 5

Quilters use contrasting colors and patterned fabric to make the pieces of a quilt block or design stand out from each other. Any color or design shape will "pop" if it is surrounded by white or black. Quilts and decorating color schemes seldom have that much white and/or black involved, so how do you use multicolored prints in the colors you want?

You need to create interesting visual effects and adequate contrast in the planning process.

You don't have to be an artist to know that color and contrast are important to your quiltmaking. You can become confident in using contrast and selecting fabrics for your quilts by learning and understanding only a few guidelines.

Usually an interesting quilt demonstrates more than one type of contrast. Not only will there be a contrast of colors, but also of print fabrics, color intensity, and the use of light and dark areas of the quilt. (**Diagram 6**) Which of the kinds of contrast do you like?

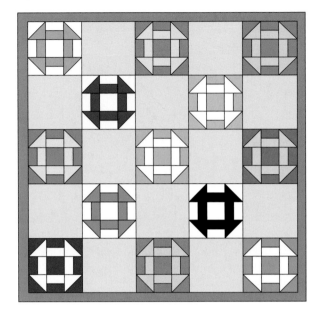

Diagram 6

Just as people have color preferences, they also have a preference as to how much contrast in value and color they prefer. For example a "high-contrast" person might prefer black and white and a "low-contrast" person might prefer gray and black or gray and white—while yet another person will like two more closely related values with almost no contrast. Neither one nor the other is more correct. No matter what your preference, the amount of contrast must be adequate to communicate the design. Are all the blocks in **Diagram 6** easy to "read"?

Color value refers to the amount of light or dark in a color. Shade refers to color that is on the darker portion of a scale. Tint refers to color that is on the lighter side of a scale. The Pure color appears in the center of the scale. The most intense bar on the scale is the Pure Hue at the center.

A good method of planning a quilt is to think of the design only in terms of value.

Remember that value/contrast is what makes the quilt design visually pleasing. (**Diagram 7**)

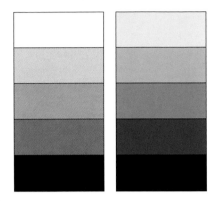

Diagram 7

Effective use of color and contrast is more an art than a science. Quilters will have their personal preference. There are no absolutes when it comes to using color. Harmonies that you will find illustrated on Color Wheels are helpful starting points for discovering your own preferences, but they are not meant to be rigid rules. The truth is that every color can be made to go with any other color, given the effective use of value and contrast. A fun way to learn about color is to find a new box of 24 crayons and play a bit.

Look through this book to see how color and visual texture is used, then make your own plans.

When in doubt go to your nearest quilt shop! They are specialist in teaching you to combine fabrics with various print scales and styles.

The most exciting part of quiltmaking and learning to select color and fabrics is that it does get easier with practice.

"Practice is the best of all instructors."

Publius Syrus

Fabric

Once you've decided on a quilt design and the general color theme of the quilt, it's time to select the fabric. Your first venture into a fabric store can either be bliss or scary—you will have so many choices. Here are just a few guidelines to get you started.

Fabrics made of 100% cotton are usually preferred by quilters. They find them easier to cut, sew, and hand quilt. Cotton fabrics also age well and they have a consistency in handling. Cotton blends can also be used if they are of equal weight, strength, weave, and stability. If you choose to use 100% cotton fabrics and blends together in the same quilt, be aware it will require extra care in cutting, sewing, and especially pressing. Check for fiber content on the ends of the bolts.

Pre-wash all fabric. All woven fabrics will have some residual shrinkage. The tightness of the weave and the quality represented by the maker's name can have some relevance to the amount of shrinkage one can expect. Wash and rinse all fabric until the water runs clear of excess dyes.

Iron the fabric to remove wrinkles. Take extra care when ironing blended cotton/polyester or other blends. Most blends are more heat sensitive than 100% cottons.

Most of the yardage you will buy will be between 41" and 44" wide. If your choice comes up short as you buy it or after you wash it you may need additional fabric. Fabric yardage listed in the Materials listing for each quilt is estimated for 44" wide fabrics.

Fabric Grain Lines

Most quilting patterns, for both patchwork and appliqué, will make note or mention of "grain line" so it's best if you know a little about the fabric you are going to use. (**Diagram 8**)

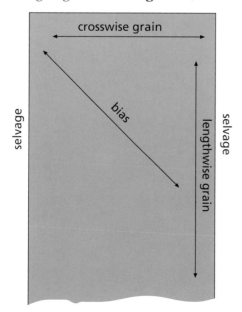

Diagram 8

The outside edges of the fabric as it comes off the bolt are called selvages. They should be trimmed away because they are more tightly woven than the rest of the fabric. If worked into the quilt, they may pull or distort the seams.

The cut edge of fabric is either stable or stretchy depending on where the cut is made.

The lengthwise grain is parallel to the edges of the selvage and is the most stable grain line. Sometimes this grain line can show the "nap" pattern, or direction of the weave.

The crosswise grain is the second-most stable grain line. Strips or pieces cut on the crosswise grain show little difference in the direction of the cut.

Lengthwise grain lines and crosswise grain lines are preferred for patchwork.

True bias is a 45-degree angle to the selvage—a diagonal line 45 degrees between the lengthwise and the crosswise grain lines. A bias-cut edge of fabric has the most stretch and must be handled carefully when cutting, sewing, and pressing.

Bias grain lines are preferred for appliqué work.

Using Scrap Fabrics

Whether you buy, reclaim, or trade your small pieces of 100% cotton fabric you can put them all into a modern quilt. Quilts made from remnants left over from clothing, decorating construction, or reclaimed from used items is probably our oldest quiltmaking tradition. There are some cautions to follow when using scraps.

Check all scraps for fiber content, color fastness, and shrinkage. If you are unsure of a scrap, wash it again. If it can't survive another washing you don't want to use it into your quilt.

Be aware of the grain line in the scrap. Pull it in several directions to make sure you are using your scrap to its best advantage.

Estimate about 20% more scrap fabric for your quilt project. Some pieces may not be a good size or fiber content.

Making and Using Templates

Selecting Template Materials

Patterns for patchwork and appliqué are given in the finished, full size—they do **not** include a seam allowance.

Thin transparent or opaque plastic is a preferred material for templates that will be used over and over. Plastic will keep its shape and the tracings will always be true each time the template is used. It can be easily cut with scissors or a craft knife.

Semi-permanent templates are also made from lightweight cardboard—our Great Grandmothers used cereal and tea boxes for their templates. Old file folders are the right weight. Fine-grit sandpaper is also used. Cardboard and sandpaper will not stand up to long-term use. They will break down and become inaccurate from wear.

Freezer paper templates are useful for pattern pieces that will be used only a few times. Freezer paper is also used to transfer the master pattern pieces to cardboard. This paper is most appropriate for appliqué templates.

Transferring Patterns to Template Material

Write all information on each pattern piece as you make it. Many will be very similar and can be easily mistaken for one another with disastrous results.

Using Plastic

Place the template plastic over the master pattern. Draw or trace the pattern pieces onto the plastic. Use a small ruler to keep the lines straight and accurate on piecing templates.

Cut out the pattern pieces with sharp scissors (Not your fabric scissors!) or a craft knife.

Using Cardboard or Sandpaper

Make a photocopy of the master pattern. Glue the copy to the cardboard or sandpaper. Cut out the pattern pieces with sharp scissors. **Bonus:** All pattern pieces will already have the information printed on it. **Caution:** *Make very sure the photocopy is accurate and not distorted in any way by the copy process.*

Tip: *Trace designs onto freezer paper. Iron the paper, shiny side down, to the cardboard or sandpaper with a warm iron. Label the pieces and cut out.*

Tip: *For home computer users, scan the master patterns onto freezer paper cut to fit your printer. Iron paper to cardboard and cut out.*

Using the Templates

Mark each piece accurately onto the wrong side of the fabric. Leave about 1/2" between each tracing. The lines you trace are the sewing lines, not the cutting lines. Add the 1/4" seam allowance by eye as you cut out each piece.

Tip: *If the fabric moves too much while being traced, place a piece of fine-grain sandpaper under the fabric to hold it firmly while tracing.*

Patchwork templates should be placed on the straight of the fabric grain. The arrows on the pattern pieces show the direction of the grain-line. This adds strength to the patchwork and increases the ease of stitching.

Appliqué templates are most often placed on the crosswise grain of the fabric. This allows the bias direction of the fabric to form more easily into the soft curves of appliqué.

Tip: *Pay close attention to overlapping and underlapping pieces in appliqué pattern pieces.* (**Diagram 9**)

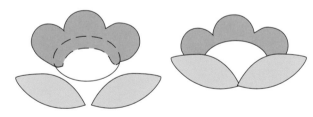

Diagram 9

Caution: *Some templates in patchwork and in appliqué have a specific direction—they are not symmetrical and can be accidentally reversed. It's a good habit to mark each template with the code "TSU" ("This Side Up") just in case a template that looks symmetrical isn't!*

Special-Use Templates

Window templates are designed to allow you to take the best advantage of your fabric, especially if you are trying to isolate a flower or other design feature in a patterned piece. You create a "window" template by using the negative space.

Trace the template shape onto a piece of cardboard or paper. Leave a couple of inches between each shape. Cut the silhouettes out with a craft knife. Clearly label the right side of the template sheet.

To use the window template, place the open shapes over the fabric and move it around until you've isolated the part of the fabric you want to use. Lightly mark around the shape using a fabric pen or pencil. (**Diagram 10**)

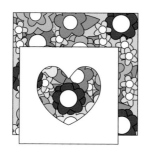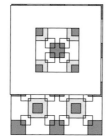

Diagram 10

Appliqué Quilts

Appliqué quilts are more easily understood than patchwork quilts because the designs are most often drawn from nature. Pieces of fabric are cut into curvilinear shapes and applied to a background fabric.

There are thousands of quilt block and quilt designs that are based on these systems and/or combinations of these systems. Make your first choices from this book and get started. It's a wonderful art!

Appliqué

Appliqué offers the quiltmaker a wider variety of decorative possibilities than traditional piecing techniques alone. It is most often used in conjunction with piecing and other embellishment techniques.

Appliqué is probably an older technique than patchwork. Appliqué as 'patching', applying a good piece over a tear, seems more useful in mending cloth and less time consuming than cutting and stitching bits of cloth together to create larger pieces of fabric as is done in piecework. In both the old and new world, skilled needle workers have used appliqué techniques as forms of mending and decoration for many centuries.

In quilts, appliqué techniques most often express the curving lines of nature, abstract designs, symbols, or other things not particularly suited to the geometric patterns of ordinary patchwork. Intricate stylized or simple realistic motifs are made by combining shapes in appliqué and embellishment techniques as in the Summertime Quilt, page 128. That small quilt has a stenciled watering can motif with appliquéd flowers. It is further embellished with embroidery.

Appliqué is done by cutting and preparing shapes from fabrics and hand or machine stitching them to a foundation fabric. The foundation fabric becomes the background for the design. The background might be a single piece of solid or print fabric or might be composed of patchwork as in the Flowers of Friendship Quilt, page 26.

Appliqué can be done by hand or machine. Either way, we use easier techniques and contemporary tools and supplies than early quiltmakers. Modern quiltmakers can pick and choose from many techniques and still feel comfortable in making a contemporary or very traditional looking hand-made quilt.

The quiltmaker of the 21st century selects from thousands of different fabric choices in every conceivable style of solid or print. One of the joys of appliqué is being able to select and use designs and fabrics that one might never use in a patchwork quilt. An added benefit is that one can build a good fabric supply in increments of $1/4$ yard or less.

Your hand appliqué projects are portable. You can whip them out and take a few stitches to pass the time or sooth your nerves when you travel the world, or at the doctor or dentist.

General Notes

Appliqué and patchwork are equal partners in quiltmaking. Although the approach and use of each technique is different they share many traits.

Most appliqué designs or patterns do not include a seam allowance. Each part of a design will require a $1/4$", sometimes a little less, seam allowance added when the pieces are cut from fabric. The raw edge of the seam allowance is turned under each piece to create a finished edge.

The stitches used to apply the appliqué pieces to the background fabric should be small, firm and close together, no more than $1/8$" apart.

All piecing seams in a project are sewn using a $1/4$" seam allowance.

Choosing Fabrics and Tools for Appliqué

Choose your fabrics carefully. Select good quality, closely woven, fabrics of 100% cotton. Fabrics that have a loose weave are not good for appliqué as they tend to easily fray and don't hold their shape. One should be able to cut the fabric cleanly with fabric scissors and not have it ravel. Custom-dyed and batik fabrics can be included. Fabrics of other fiber content might be used by experienced needleworkers. Choose your appliqué fabrics for good contrast and interesting visual texture. There should be enough contrast between the background fabrics and the pieces being applied to clearly communicate the design. Needle workers, who favor appliqué, are constantly looking for fabrics that add contrast, dimension, and interest to their work.

The following is a list of needed or useful tools and supplies. Before beginning a project, buy the basic supplies: good fabric, needles, thread, scissors, and a good needle threader. As you work you will discover for yourself any additional supplies or tools you need. Each technique might require specific supply needs, so buy on an as-needed basis.

Hand Needles: Use the proper needle for successful appliqué. A sharp is the class of needle you will use. Sharps are long, thin, and somewhat flexible needles designed for hand stitching and appliqué. It is also the common needle used for hand piecing quilts. The points and eyes of these needles are long and very thin. Look at the eye of the needle and buy the one you feel you can thread by "eye" or with the help of a needle threader. If you can't thread it, you can't use it.

Appliqué Pins: These pins are 1" to $1^1/2$", thin and very sharp. They have very small glass heads or flat disk-shaped heads.

Bias Bars and Bias Tape Makers: These are used for making smooth stems, vines and reed shapes for woven appliqué. The bars can be found in a wide variety of widths and manufactured in aluminum or in heat-resistant plastic. The bias tape makers are manufactured in fewer widths but they might be easier to find. These tools have set the standard for uniform and flowing stems and vines.

Facings: Nylon tulle and lightweight interfacings are used for quick turning of large, simple appliqué shapes. Do not use the fusible facings for appliqué.

Freezer Paper: Coated paper used as a foundation for appliqué and for making cardboard templates. Find this product at the grocery store.

Glue Stick or Liquid Starch: Used to hold seam allowance in place before or while stitching.

Hemostats or Long Tweezers: For pulling the needle or removing template materials - also good for holding and turning small parts of the appliqué.

Marking Pens and Pencils for Fabric: Use rinse-out markers, silver or white pencils, soap slivers or a variety of other non-permanent markers for dark and light fabrics. Do not use waxy dressmaker pencils. Mark fabrics with a very light touch when working with these tools so they can easily be removed from the fabric.

Markers for Template Material: Permanent, fine-pointed black markers to create permanent, accurate lines on template materials.

Needle Grabber: Use a rubber finger tip or disk to help grip small needles and pins. A rubber balloon will work in a pinch.

Needle Threader: A tool designed with a very fine wire to pass through the eye of a needle and catch the thread.

Rulers and Tape Measure: Ruler: 1" x 6" and yard stick. Used for centering designs and for general measuring of the quilt and its parts.

Scissors: Fabric and paper scissors are needed. Small, sharp-pointed, embroidery scissors are useful for detail work.

Spray Starch or Sizing: Use sparingly to add body to pre-washed fabrics.

Stencils and French Curves: Circle stencils and French curves are made of plastic. They are useful in creating perfect circles and gentle curves. They are available in office supply stores and some quilt shops.

Template Materials: Choose heat-resistant materials for appliqué templates when possible. Cardboard, file folders, poster-board or Mylar™ are good choices. Template plastic is good, but not heat resistant.

Thimble: A well-fitting thimble is suggested for all hand stitching. The thimble should be snug without pinching or applying pressure on the finger joint. It is most commonly worn on the middle finger of the dominant hand.

Thread: Appliqué thread should be fine and of good quality. The color of thread should match the fabric piece being applied. Cotton or silk are good choices. Taupe and medium grey are good neutrals for use with many similarly-colored fabrics. Hand embroidery threads and floss should be used for decorative work only and not to apply the appliqué pieces to the background.

Wooden Toothpicks: Toothpicks should be strong and smooth. These are used to help turn appliqué seam allowances under for easier stitching and control of the seam allowance.

Preparing the Appliqué Pieces

There are many good techniques for preparing the pieces of fabric for hand appliqué. Ask six needleworkers who enjoy appliqué, and you will discover they might use half-a-dozen—or more—similar techniques, but, they might each use them under different circumstances or in different ways.

That's the art of appliqué—knowing when and how to use different techniques. Several good techniques are offered in this book. As you become more interested in the art of appliqué you may want to explore others and add them to your repertoire.

The techniques offered here are those I suggest for beginning and intermediate quiltmakers. They are almost "no-fail" techniques that are forgiving and allow one to easily correct most mistakes. I'm not a beginner and these techniques are some I prefer to use and to teach most often. As you practice you might even invent some useful

technique yourself—this is an art that lends itself to inspiration and enlivens the imagination.

Basic Freezer Paper Techniques

1. Trace around the appliqué template onto the dull side of the freezer paper.

2. Cut the actual shape from the paper. Do not add a seam allowance.

3. Pin the paper piece to the wrong side of the fabric with the dull side down.

4. Using a sharp hard pencil or stylus, trace around the template creasing the seam allowance fold line. Cut the fabric around the shape leaving a scant 1/4" seam allowance.

Tip: *If the appliqué fabric is too soft after washing, use spray starch or sizing to add a little crispness or body to the fabric.*

5. Clip into the seam allowance almost to the creased line. Clip only the inside curves and "V" areas. (**Diagram 11**) Clip as little as possible.

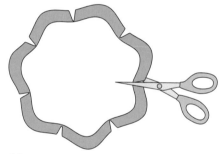

Diagram 11

6. With the point of a hot iron, press the seam allowances over the edge of the paper. The heat will stick the fabric to the shiny side of the freezer paper. Move along the seam allowance edge carefully to create smooth curves and crisp points. (**Diagram 12**)

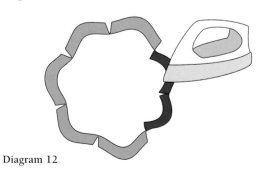

Diagram 12

Tip: *Use a smaller, lightweight travel iron to press seam allowances to the freezer paper. I find I can control this iron better for the delicate edges of appliqué.*

Alternate Methods

Method 1: Instead of using an iron to fuse the fabric to the freezer paper you can use a fabric glue stick to fasten the fabric to the paper. Use a light touch with the glue stick and smooth the fabric to make the proper curves and points. (**Diagram 13**)

Diagram 13

Method 2: Fold the seam allowance over the edge of the freezer paper and baste the seam allowance down using needle and thread. (**Diagram 14**)

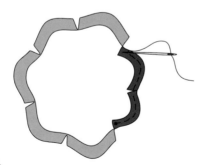

Diagram 14

Method 3: The needle-turn technique is an advanced technique made easier with freezer paper. Prepare the freezer paper as for the other techniques. With a warm iron, press the shiny side of the paper shape onto the right side of the fabric. Cut the shape from fabric leaving a scant 1/4" seam allowance. Pin the shape to the background

fabric. Use your sewing needle to turn the seam allowance under the edge of the paper then stitch the piece in place. You turn only about a quarter inch of fabric under at one time. (**Diagram 15**)

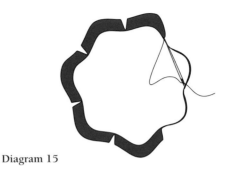

Diagram 15

Tip: *Draw once—Cut many! For several pieces of the same symmetrical shape, cut a strip of freezer paper the general height of the appliqué template. Draw shape onto the dull side of paper. Accordion-fold the paper to fit the piece. Staple the folded paper together to keep it from slipping. Cut out shape. Keep shapes stapled together and pull off the back of the pile as needed. (**Diagram 16**)*

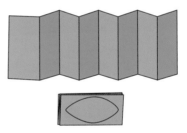

Diagram 16

Tip: *No matter which method you choose, place appliqué pieces in a plastic baggie until you are ready to use them.*

Some Special Techniques

Appliqué is very forgiving as a needle technique, but there are a few firm guidelines to follow—circles should be smooth, curved lines should be curves, pointed leaves should remain pointed and stems and vines should be of even width and appear to move or grow gracefully.

The good thing about these guidelines is that even a beginner can quickly learn the skills it takes to follow them.

Pointed Leaves

Using the Freezer Paper technique, press the seam allowance over the paper—first one side and then the other. (**Diagram 17**)

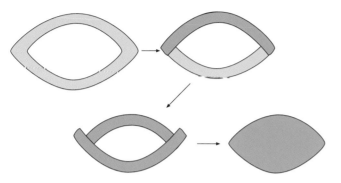

Diagram 17

Do not cut off excess fabric tags at the ends of leaf. Roll this tag of seam allowance fabric under the leaf just before you stitch it down. Use a toothpick or stylus. Sometimes a little touch of a glue stick will help hold it under until you stitch.

Perfect Circles

Using the Freezer Paper technique, page 149, and a perfect template, cut circles.

Method 1: Pin freezer paper circle shiny side up, onto the wrong side of fabric. Trim seam allowance to a scant $1/4$". Carefully press the seam allowance over the paper with a hot iron. (**Diagram 18**)

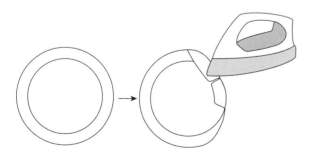

Diagram 18

Method 2: Make a fabric circle about 1" larger than the freezer-paper circle. Stitch $1/8$" from the outside edge of the fabric circle. Place the freezer-paper circle in the center of the fabric and draw up fabric around the paper. Make a knot and press. (**Diagram 19**)

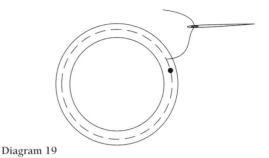

Diagram 19

Stacked Designs

Many appliqué patterns have multiple layers built up over just one foundation piece. Flowers and butterflies come to mind. Place the smaller parts (with the smallest on top) onto the larger piece and stitch to the larger piece. Stitch the appliqué composite onto the background fabric. (**Diagram 20**)

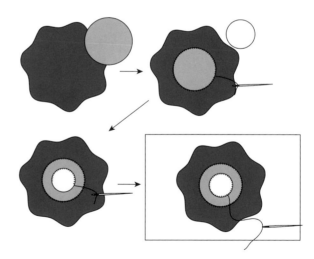

Diagram 20

Making Bias Strips

Flowing lines like stems, vines, or butterfly antenna are best made with bias strips. The flowing stems in the "Flowers of Friendship" quilt, page 26, are good examples of these techniques.

1. Fold a corner of fabric over to make a 45-degree angle; finger press a fold.

2. Open the fabric and cut along the fold.

3. Determine the width of bias strips needed following the pattern or the manufacturer's guidelines for the width of strip you will need. Then cut strips using the first cut edge as a guide. (**Diagram 21**)

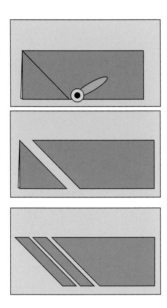

Diagram 21

Tip: *You will need to experiment with the bias strip width. Your stitching habits will ultimately determine the size strips you will need to use.*

4. Join cut strips to form a longer strip, sewing along the short ends. (**Diagram 22**) Press seams open and cut off points.

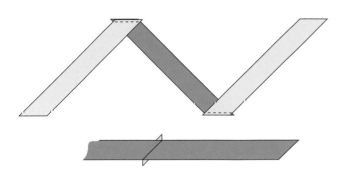

Diagram 22

Using Bias Bars

Bias bars are made from metal or heat-resistant plastic. They come in a variety of widths from 1/8" to 1".

1. Press bias strip in half lengthwise with wrong sides together, then make a line of machine or hand stitching two or three threads wider than the bias bar. This creates the bias tube.

2. Trim excess fabric close to stitching. Place bias bar into the tube and slip the seam line around to the underside of bar. (**Diagram 23**)

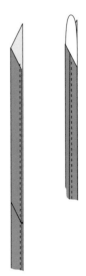

Diagram 23

3. Spray starch on the front and press with an iron. Slip bar further through the fabric tube and continue pressing.

4. Wrap the finished bias tube around an old spool or a piece of cardboard until you are ready to use it.

Preparing the Background Fabric for Appliqué

Cut the background fabric to the size required for your block or project. Remember it must have the seam allowance included.

Tip: *Make a cardboard template the exact size of your finished block. Using this template, and a fabric marker, outline the block on the wrong side of the background fabric. Cut the background fabric leaving a generous seam allowance. When the block or piece has been appliquéd, cut the background allowing a true 1/4" seam allowance around all sides of the block.*

Press or lightly mark centering lines on the background fabric. Draw similar lines on the master appliqué design or on a copy of the master design. This will give you placement guidelines for each of the appliqué elements. (**Diagram 24**)

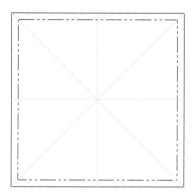

Diagram 24

Making an Overlay

This is an additional method of making sure you place your appliqué pieces correctly. Place a piece of clear plastic (like a plastic sheet protector) over the appliqué design. Tape the plastic to the design to prevent it from slipping. Trace the design onto the plastic using a permanent marking pen. (**Diagram 25**)

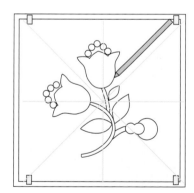

Diagram 25

Using the Overlay

Pin marked overlay to prepared background fabric. Use a ruler to make sure sides of the design are of equal distance from edges of block outline.

Slip the prepared appliqué pieces under the overlay—position them correctly under the plastic and pin in place until you are ready to remove the overlay and stitch.

Tip: *Baste the appliqué pieces to the background if the appliqué project will take more than a single sitting to finish or if you plan to take the project with you.*

Appliqué Stitches

There are several types of stitches for hand appliqué. Each has its own merit. There are four common styles of utility hand stitches – Invisible stitch, Whipstitch, Topstitch, and Broderie Perse technique. A Blanket stitch technique is often used as a decorative stitch over a seam allowance.

The Invisible Stitch

The Invisible Stitch is made at $1/8"$ maximum intervals through the side fold of the seam allowance. It is a hidden stitch.

Push the needle through the seam allowance fold from the backside to hide the thread knot; pull the needle through the background fabric. Next, push the needle through the background fabric even to the place where the needle came out. Advance the needle about $1/16"$ to $1/8"$ along the backside—repeat for the next stitch. (**Diagram 26**)

Diagram 26

A little tug after each stitch secures the thread. This stitch is most commonly preferred by quilters making heirloom-quality appliqué quilts and it takes a little practice to perfect. (**Diagram 27**)

Right Side   Under Side

Diagram 27

The Whipstitch

The Whipstitch is an older style of appliqué stitch. Some quilters prefer this stitch as they feel it is easier and faster than the Invisible Stitch. This stitch is made at ⅛" intervals through the bottom and top of the seam allowance; it will be visible on the appliquéd piece. (**Diagram 28**) Because this

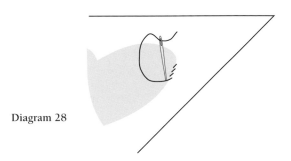

Diagram 28

stitch secures the appliqué piece through two layers, it creates a strong bond with the background fabric. Since the appliquéd piece is secured more firmly, the seam is well protected making this stitch a good choice for appliqué quilts that are expected to see much use. (**Diagram 29**)

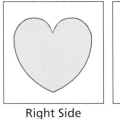

Right Side   Under Side

Diagram 29

The Topstitch

The Topstitch is quicker than either the Invisible stitch or the Whipstitch. The stitch is made at ⅛" to ¼" intervals through the bottom and the top seam allowance of the appliquéd piece, about 1/16" from the fold. (**Diagram 30**)

Right Side   Under Side

Diagram 30

Because this stitch secures the appliqué piece through three layers—top, seam allowance and backing—it creates a strong bond. The appearance of the stitch is more decorative than either of the other appliqué stitches. It is an excellent choice for contemporary appliqué. Use of the Topstitch for appliqué was revived by Jean Ray Laury in the mid 1950s on "Tom's Quilt." This particular quilt has had a significant influence on contemporary appliqué quiltmaking.

Blanket Stitch

The Blanket stitch gives a decorative finished edge to appliqué that has already been anchored by a utility stitch. (**Diagram 31**) It is used in contemporary appliqué, but it was especially popular in the 1930s. It's used on the Butterflies quilt, page 8.

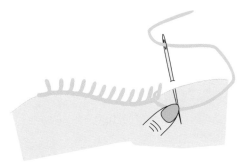

Diagram 31

Broderie Perse Stitch

This is both a utility and a decorative stitch. It is created as a small, close, Blanket-style stitch over the raw edge of applied fabric. The edge of the appliqué pieces are pre-treated with an anti-fraying product to prevent raveling of cut edges. The short stitches joining the appliqué to the background fabric are made very close together and resemble a very fine machine zigzag stitch. (**Diagram 32**)

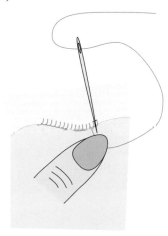

Diagram 32

154

During the 18th century, when floral cloth was very expensive and difficult to come by, needleworkers made a practice of cutting out the printed flowers and other elements from costly goods. They did not allow for a seam allowance. In this way the printed designs could be spread out to cover a much larger area. The edges of the fabric would be treated with laundry starch or rabbit skin glue to protect the edge before and after working the Broderie Perse.

Even though these, and other stitches are used and useful in appliqué today, they have a long history in the craft and tradition.

The stitches must be small and attach the piece firmly to the background fabric no matter which technique you choose.

After stitching a piece in place, remove the pins or basting threads.

Next, cut away part of the background fabric that lies under the patch to reveal the paper. Do not cut too close to your stitching.

Use tweezers or your fingers to remove the paper pattern.

Tip: *Press appliqué work from the backside first and then from the top. A soft ironing board surface is preferred for appliqué. Place a thin bath towel on an ironing board and cover it with a piece of muslin for the desired softness.*

The Stenciled Quilt

Stenciling has a long history as a decorative art and technique. Often used in architecture, pottery, and home decoration, it's not surprising to find a strong tradition of stenciled fabrics in quilts.

The stenciled quilt is a vital form in American quilt history. Making stenciled summer bedcovers and quilts was a popular pastime in the first quarter of the nineteenth century. The stencil paints, dyes, brushes and stencil patterns used for fabric were often the same as were used on walls, floors, furniture and other home accessories.

Basic stenciling techniques have changed little over the centuries. However, life is easier for the modern practice of fabric stenciling. The fabric paints and dyes are permanent and simplified techniques make stenciling a lot of fun. It's not surprising that stenciling techniques are becoming more and more evident in contemporary quilts. The Whig Rose quilt (page 100) which is stenciled, appliquéd and pieced, is a contemporary approach to a traditional quilt style.

Supplies Needed For Fabric Stenciling

Pre-washed Fabrics: prints or solids.

Permanent Fabric Paints or Dyes: Versatex is a very easy-to-use emulsified permanent paint.

Stencil Brushes: stiff short bristle brushes. One brush is necessary for each color.

Stencil Sponge Brushes: used for special effects.

Craft Knife or Small Sharp Scissors: for cutting stencil mask.

Freezer Paper: used for creating the stencil to mask the paint. Very thin plastic can also be used as the mask.

Plastic-coated Paper Plate: use as a paint palette.

Fine-grade Sandpaper: use to keep fabric from slipping.

Yardstick and Pencil or Fabric Marker: for marking fabric.

Rotary Cutting Mat or Thick Magazine: to protect a table from craft knife.

Preparing the Fabric

Wash all fabric to remove extra dyes and sizing. Press the fabric without using sizing or starch. This makes the fabric more receptive to the stenciling paints and techniques.

Planning the Quilt or Project

Cut the fabric 2" larger than the finished project. Use a yardstick or ruler to mark guidelines on the fabric for the project. Stencil paint is highly concentrated and will stain the fabric even before heat setting. Guidelines will help prevent stenciling mistakes.

Practice

Practice the stenciling technique to help you understand the principle of painting with a stencil.

Cut a 3" x 3" square of freezer paper. Fold square in half and using scissors or a craft knife, cut a heart in the middle of the square. (**Diagram 33**)

Diagram 33

You've just created a paper stencil that will mask and protect the fabric while you stencil the heart. This simple stencil can create any number of designs. (**Diagram 34**)

Diagram 34

Place the freezer paper stencil, shiny side down, in the center of the right side of a scrap of fabric. With a warm iron, press the stencil onto the fabric. This will help to keep the paint from creeping under the stencil.

Work a small amount of paint into a stencil brush by touching the tip of the brush into the paint. Next swirl the brush over the paper plate palette to remove much of the paint and to work the paint into all the ends of the stencil brush. Excess paint can be brushed off onto paper towels if necessary. The technique is called a "dry-brush" technique the brush should be almost dry before you touch it to the stencil.

Begin stenciling by brushing in a clockwise motion on the paper stencil and slowly over the open edges of the cut-out heart shape. The motion should start over the edge of the design slowly adding paint to the fabric. Work with a light to medium pressure on the brush. The brush can also be tapped over the fabric area. (**Diagram 35**)

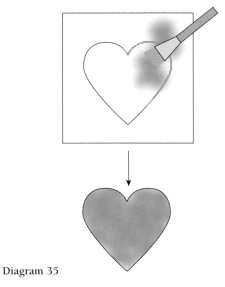

Diagram 35

Tip: *Working with too much paint on the brush or too heavy a hand will cause the paint to be pushed under the paper mask and spoil your work. Apply the paint a little at a time. You can always more—but you can't take it away.*

Tip: *If the fabric moves around too much while you are stenciling, place a piece of fine sandpaper under it to help hold it in place.*

Making Design Stencils

Most stencil designs will have more than one color. Therefore, a freezer paper stencil is cut for each color. Cut pieces of freezer paper the size of the block or border to be stenciled—you will need one for each color that is in the block. Mark the dull side of the paper with guidelines for centering the design and registering the next color. (**Diagram 36**)

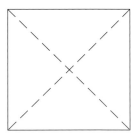

Diagram 36

As an example, look at the way the paper stencils are marked and cut for the stencils in Summertime, page 130. (**Diagram 37**) Trace the parts of the design that will be of one color. Mark these parts with a permanent marker. With a pencil, trace over other design elements to aid in placing the other stencils. Repeat these steps for each color that will be used.

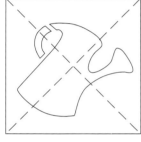

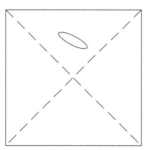

Diagram 37

Tip: *Instead of tracing the design, make as many photocopies of the original design as the number of colors or the number of stencils to be cut. Lightly color in the individual parts for a single color and repeat for each color.*

Cutting the Stencils

Tip: *Cut more than one stencil per color on the chance that one stencil is torn or ruined while painting.*

Layer the marked freezer paper over the dull side of a blank sheet of freezer paper. Pin or staple the sheets together. If using the photocopy technique place it over the freezer paper sheets and pin or staple them together.

Use a craft knife or very sharp, small scissors to cut out only those areas to be painted in that color. After making all the necessary cuts, make sure each stencil is marked with any notations needed to line up the next color accurately. Continue using these techniques for each color to be stenciled. (**Diagram 38**)

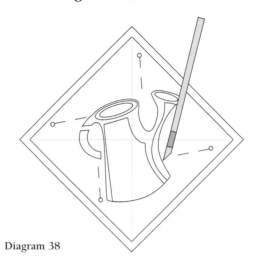

Diagram 38

Tip: *If using a craft knife you must also protect the surface under the freezer paper from being cut—a rotary mat is good for this.*

Tip: *Use various sizes of hole punches or scrapbook punches for interesting small details in your stencil designs.*

Cutting Mirror Image Stencils

It's easy to create a mirror image stencil for borders or designs you want to face each other. When you layer your freezer paper sheets to cut multiples, layer the sheets in pairs. The pair is created by placing two sheets together with the shiny sides facing each other. Staple or pin the layers and cut the stencil as usual. (**Diagram 39**)

Diagram 39

Making the Stenciled Designs Permanent

Most fabric paints and dyes require some type of heat to set the colors. Follow the instructions provided by the paint manufacturer.

Hand Piecing Techniques

Piecing quilt patches by hand is a relaxing and very portable activity. It's especially comforting to have some handwork around while having to wait in airports or for an appointment—it is as if we are salvaging those fragments of time that otherwise might seem frustrating and lost to us.

The beauty of patchwork is that it is small and can be tucked into a pocket, purse, or briefcase and brought out for work as needed. Plastic baggies are perfect for transporting handwork. The smart patchworker always keeps a plastic baggie ready with a small project or block, needle, thread, needle threader (if necessary), and something with which to cut the thread.

Tip: *Using the cutter from an empty dental floss container is perfect to use when traveling.*

The techniques for making patchwork are easy to learn and to do. The stitch is a simple Running stitch using a sharp needle and a knotted length of common thread—and with a couple of pins to hold your patches in place as you work, you are ready to go.

Cutting the Pieces

Lay the template with the labels up onto the wrong side of the fabric. Place the templates for the best use of the fabric. Always allow about ¹/₂" between each template for the seam allowances. (**Diagram 40**)

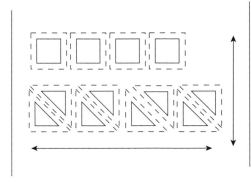

Diagram 40

Trace around the template holding a pencil or marker at a 90-degree angle to the fabric—this is for accuracy. Continue moving the templates over the fabric and marking the necessary lines. The lines you are marking are your sewing lines. Pay close attention to the direction of the grain line.

Tip: *Mark the points clearly. You need to know the starting and stopping points when stitching.*

Cut out the fabric patch leaving a ¹/₄" seam allowance around each piece. In the beginning you might want to use a small plastic ruler and mark an accurate ¹/₄" seam allowance. Do this until you can trust your judgment.

Tip: *Remember—the first traced line is the most important as it is the stitching line. It must be accurate or your patches will not go together correctly. A few errors, multiplied over just a few seams, can mean disaster as you try to put together the larger pieces and blocks.*

Tip: *If you are cutting many pieces from the same template, you can make a template that includes the seam allowance. To use this oversized template, create many layers of the needed fabric before tracing the template onto the top piece of fabric (wrong sides up). Pin the stack together. Cut the multiple layers with sharp dressmakers scissors or with a rotary cutter, ruler and mat. Accuracy is very important. Lay the normal template within each of the mass-cut fabric shapes and trace the seam lines on the wrong side of each piece.* (**Diagram 41**)

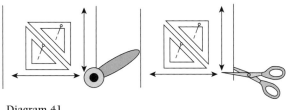

Diagram 41

Tip: *If you are cutting many of the same size and shape, you can keep them all together in a plastic baggie or string them together with needle and thread.* (**Diagram 42**)

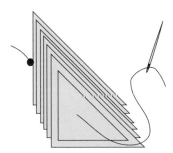

Diagram 42

Sewing the Patches

After you have cut out all the block patches and before you begin to stitch, it is a good idea to lay out all the pieces. It may look like the pieces won't fit together correctly especially if your block contains a lot of triangles. (**Diagram 43**) What you are seeing as excess fabrics are your seam allowances—you need those!

Diagram 43

Tip: *Some quilters like to have a piece of white or gray flannel for use in laying out their patchwork. A few straight pins will secure the patches. The flannel can be rolled up and put way without disturbing your work. A piece of flannel about 18" x 18" will do for all but your largest projects.*

To begin sewing, pick up the first patches and pin together at the end points. Make sure the pins are placed through the points on each patch. You will find yourself flipping the patches from front to back several times as you work. These are the only two pins you need to use unless the patches are large. (**Diagram 44**)

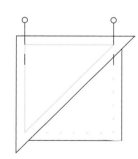

Diagram 44

Stitching

Thread a sharp needle with about an 18" length of thread. Put a knot at one end. The patches are stitched with a single thread. Start stitching about ¼" from one end towards the point. Stitch to the point and reverse, stitching across the seam to the opposite point. Before you make a knot you will want to reverse your stitching and stitch back about ¼". Then make a small knot on the seam line and cut off the thread. (**Diagram 45**) This method reinforces the seams at the end points.

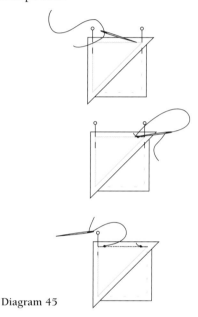

Diagram 45

When joining seamed patches together, the previously joined seam should not be stitched into the new seam. To keep it free and flexible you will pass the needle through the old seam and continue on with the remaining part of the new seam. If you want to secure this area a bit, sew a small Backstitch on either side of the flexible seam to reinforce the area. (**Diagram 46**)

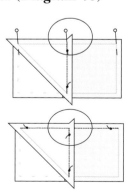

Diagram 46

Flexible seam allowances allow for hand-stitched seams to be pressed toward the darker patch even when it would be impossible or much more difficult had the seam been machine stitched. This is one reason many quiltmakers prefer hand piecing some of the very complicated patches—there is flexibility in the work that isn't present otherwise.

Curved Seam Piecing

Don't be intimidated by curved seam blocks. They are much easier than they appear and they definitely add a "wow" factor to your finished work.

Begin as you would for straight seam piecing. Place right sides together and place a pin at the beginning and the end of the seam. A pin or two can be placed at midpoint. Try not to over-pin the curved seam. (**Diagram 47**) Don't clip any of the curves. The natural ease of the curved bias edges should allow enough give for the seam.

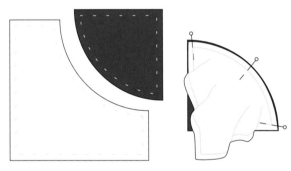

Diagram 47

As you make your running stitches, look back and forth between the front and back of the seam. Use your fingers to ease the seam edges together and to create a smooth seam line. Don't be discouraged—it does take practice.

Tip: *The seam allowance will probably lie toward the outer curved piece as it is stitched. Press toward the inclination of the curved seam allowance even if it is the lighter patch. If the dark edge of the seam allowance shows on the right side of the joined pieces, you will want to slightly trim back the darker seam allowance to eliminate seeing it.*

Unit Construction and Sewing Inset Seams

One of the first questions a new quiltmaker asks is "How do I know what to sew together first?"

After only a little practice, the blocks and whole quilt designs will be easier to read. Quilters learn to break down a block or quilt design into easier sub-units. Learning to see, understand, and use these sub-units not only make it easier to put together a block or quilt but, also to remember the design and overall pattern. Just think of it as learning the fun-filled new "language" of quiltmaking.

Thinking in Units

Look at the following figures of common quilt blocks and the way they are broken into units and sub-units. (**Diagram 48**) Some blocks are more complicated than others, but all traditional quilt blocks can be easily understood by the experienced quiltmaker. Remember the quote by Publius Syrus, "Practice is the best of all instructors."

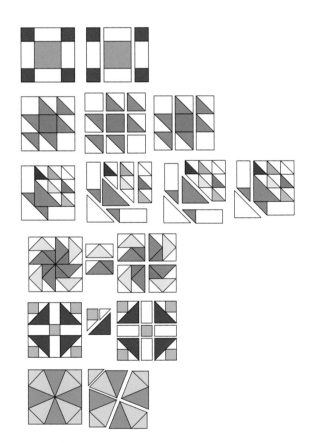

Diagram 48

Sewing Inset Seams

Some patches cannot go together with one continuous straight seam. The patches are inset when two pieces come together along non-parallel edges. (**Diagram 49**) Pin at the end points and at the pivot points as you stitch.

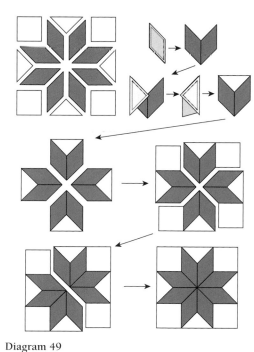

Diagram 49

Tip: *All straight edge piecing techniques still apply. Stitch the seams from the innermost point toward the outer edge of the block. (**Diagram 50**).*

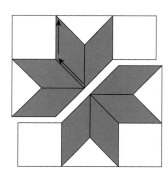

Diagram 50

Finishing Up

It's all in the details! You've got your blocks stitched and now you are ready to finish up…

Squaring the Blocks

Before you sew any blocks together, check to make sure they are the same size. If all blocks in a project are supposed to be 6" x 6" when finished, they should all measure 6½" x 6½" before they are put into the quilt.

Measure all blocks and square them up to the same size. Remember that you must leave the ¼" seam allowance all around the block. If a block is quite out-of-square then a trim might be necessary or you might need to rip a few seams out and re-stitch them to get the block square.

Tip: *A quick and inexpensive way to check if a block is square is to cut a piece of computer paper the exact size the block should be including the seam allowance. You could also cut a piece of template plastic to the correct size—or buy a large, square acrylic ruler.*

Horizontal Rows

1. Lay out the blocks in the correct arrangement. (**Diagram 51**)

Diagram 51

2. Stack all the blocks of the first row and pin a piece of paper to the top block with the #1 written on it. Repeat for all rows (**Diagram 52**)

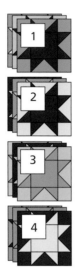

Diagram 52

3. Sew the first row of blocks together and press all the seams in one direction. Pick up the next row and sew the blocks together. Press the seams in the opposite direction from the first row. Sew each row alternating the direction of the seams. (**Diagram 53**)

Diagram 53

Diagonal Sets

1. Lay out the diagonal rows in the correct arrangement. (**Diagram 54**)

Diagram 54

2. Stack all the blocks in each row and label each row as in step 2 of Horizontal Rows.

3. Sew the first row of blocks together and press all the seams in one direction. Pick up the next row, sew the blocks together. and press seams in the opposite direction. Sew each row alternating the direction of the seams.

Finishing Triangles

Setting and Corner Triangles for Diagonal Sets

Setting Triangles are placed at the top, bottom, and sides of blocks that are set together on the diagonal. The easiest way to create finishing triangles is to start with a square. To calculate the size of the square needed to create the correct size of the triangles, multiply the size of your finished block by 1.414 and add $1\frac{1}{4}$" for seam allowances.

Cut the square into quarter triangles. Note the grain line directions on the triangles. Measure $\frac{1}{4}$" inside each triangle to create the seam allowance guideline. These lines are shown as stitching lines in **Diagram 55**.

Diagram 55

162

Example: 3" block x 1.414 = 4.242…next add 1.25 (1¼")…this equals 5.492". Round up the last number. Your starting square, to create the correct triangle size is 5.5" x 5.5" (5½" x 5½").

Corner Triangles are placed at the corners of the diagonally set quilt blocks. The easiest way to create these corner triangles is to start with a square. To calculate the size of the square needed to create the correct size of these triangles you will divide the size of your finished block by 1.414 and add .875" (⅞") for seam allowance.

Cut this square in half on the diagonal to create two right, 90-degree triangles. Note the grain line directions on the triangles. Measure ¼" inside each triangle to create the seam allowance guideline. These lines are shown as stitching lines in **Diagram 56**.

Diagram 56

Example: 3" block ÷ 1.414 = 2.121…next add .875"…this equals 2.996". Round this number up to 3".

The starting square is 3" x 3" for the Corner triangles.

Setting Squares

Many diagonally set quilts have plain blocks set between the pieced or appliquéd blocks. To calculate the size of the square needed, you simply add ½" to the size of the pieced or appliquéd block.

Example: A 3" pieced block, before it is set into the quilt, actually should measure 3½" x 3½". The seemingly extra size is made up of the needed seam allowances. So, to calculate the cut size of a setting square, use the size of the finished square and add the seam allowance (¼") to each side of the square.

Note: *These are the techniques used to calculate the measurements needed for the Setting Squares and Triangles in the Shoo-Fly quilt (page 122) and the Red Nine-Patch quilt (page 54).*

Adding Borders

Think of borders as the frame of the quilt. Pay close attention to the border design and the selection of fabric. For the sake of unity it's a good idea to repeat a fabric or color that is in the body of the quilt.

Prepare the top for borders by making sure the sides, top and bottom, and corners are square and trim. Press the quilt top. Take five measurements on the quilt. Trim to square if necessary. **(Diagram 57)**

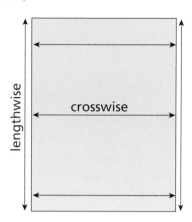

lengthwise

crosswise

Diagram 57

Simple Borders

1. Cut and piece (if necessary) border strips to match the crosswise quilt top measurement.

Note: *Piece strips on the diagonal; trim about ¼" from stitching. Press seams open to reduce bulk.* **(Diagram 58)**

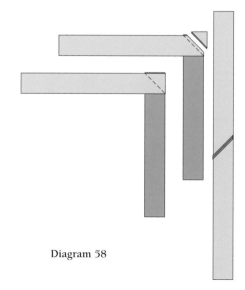

Diagram 58

2. Pin borders to the top and bottom edges of the quilt. Sew these borders to the quilt and press seams toward the borders. (**Diagram 59**)

Diagram 59

3. Cut and piece border strips to match lengthwise quilt measurement including the top and bottom borders.

4. Pin the borders to the sides of the quilt, sew to quilt and press seams toward the borders. (**Diagram 60**)

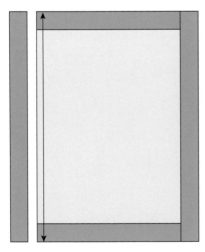

Diagram 60

For additional simple borders repeat steps 1 through 4.

Borders with Cornerstones

1. Cut and piece (if necessary) the border strips to the exact length of the top and bottom and the sides of the quilt. (**Diagram 61**)

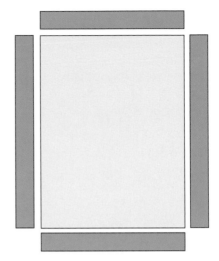

Diagram 61

2. Pin the top and bottom strips to the quilt body and sew in place. Press this seam toward the outside of the quilt.

3. Cut four squares the exact size as the width of the border strips. Sew these squares to the ends of the side border strips. Press these seams toward the border strips. Sew finished border units to the sides of the quilt body. (**Diagram 62**)

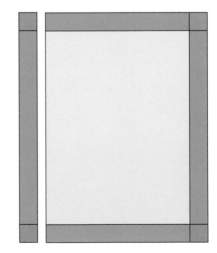

Diagram 62

Mitered Borders
An Advanced Technique

1. Cut and piece (if necessary) all the border strips diagonally. (See **Diagram 58**, page 163.)

2. Calculate the length of the top and bottom strips:

Width of quilt_____+ 2 x width of border strip + 4" = Length of top and bottom strip. (Example: 45" + 2 x 6" + 4 = 61")

3. Pin and sew these border strips to the top and bottom beginning and ending $^1/_4$" from each end. (**Diagram 63**)

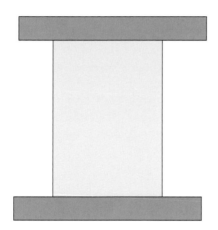

Diagram 63

4. Calculate the length of the side strips:

Length of quilt_____+ 2 x width of border strips + 4" = Length of side strips. (Example: 60" + 2 x 6" + 4 = 76")

5. Pin and sew the lengthwise strips to the sides of the quilt, stopping at the seam allowance of the top and bottom borders. (**Diagram 64**)

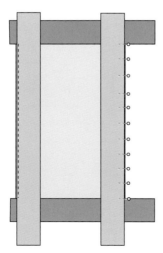

Diagram 64

6. Lift the side border piece and fold it under itself at a 45-degree angle. (**Diagram 65**) Use a ruler or a square of paper folded in half diagonally to make sure it is an accurate 45-degree angle. Pin the two border pieces together on the underside and press to set the fold line.

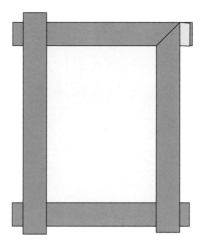

Diagram 65

7. Stitch the borders together using the fold line as a guide. Trim off excess fabric about $^1/_4$" from stitching line. (**Diagram 66**) Press seam open.

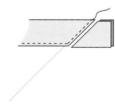

Diagram 66

Hand Quilting

Hand quilting can be one of the most relaxing and enjoyable of all needlework. Learning to relax and enjoy the process is the key. Some quilters liken the repetitive motion to a form of meditation. Others will admit that it is a pleasant time spent gathering feelings and thoughts. One of the best things about hand quilting is that it is completely portable.

The idea of hand quilting steps beyond the simple utility of stitching together the three layers of a quilt. The art of hand quilting endures because nothing can duplicate the look of fine hand quilting. It is the defining hallmark of the elegance of this fine craft. Today, nearly all quilters save hand quilting for their finest patchwork and appliqué projects.

The largest number of quilts in the 20th and the 21st centuries are hand quilted using a short running stitch. This is the same, slightly modified, stitch used for hand piecing. Quilt collectors and very traditional quiltmakers look for a different type of stitch that is the hallmark of the finest 18th-, 19th- and 20th-century quilts—the Dimple stitch.

Whichever way it is accomplished, the hand quilting stitch is a small running-style stitch that holds the three layers of the quilt sandwich together. The stitch is done with a short strong needle called a "between." The higher the number listed on the package of needles, the smaller the needle. When learning to make the hand quilting stitch, one might begin working with a size 9 needle. With practice one can expect to progress to a size 10 or 12.

General Supplies for Hand Quilting

Supplies for hand quilting are few and basic. These can be found in any quilt or general fabric shop.

Between Needles: In various sizes: 9, 10, 12.

Quilting Thread: Cotton or cotton/polyester hard-twist varieties are available in many colors.

Thimble: A thimble should be worn on the middle finger of your dominant hand. It should fit without falling off or being too tight against the knuckle. The thimble should have deep dimples. A thimble is a necessity for hand quilting.

Finger Cots: Also called secretary's rubber fingers and are used for aiding in pulling the needle through the layers.

Needle Threader: These are helpful in threading the eye of smaller needles.

Scissors: Small scissors used for embroidery.

Marking Pencils and Pens: Should be removable by washing or erasing and should not damage the fabric. These can be water-soluble pens, pencils or chalks.

Masking Tape: Use quick or easy-release tapes in various widths as stitching guides for straight lines.

Ruler and Yardstick: Used for marking quilting lines and centering design motifs.

Quilting Stencils: Are bought or made for creating quilting designs.

Hoops and Frames: Are used to stretch and keep the quilt layers from shifting while stitching. For portable projects use 4" to 6" hoops that can be placed in a plastic baggie with your piecing or appliqué. Hoops and frames are most commonly made of wood or plastic and come in a wide variety of sizes and styles. Buy for quality and long-term use. For home use, I suggest a 14" or 16" wooden or plastic hoop.

Batting: The warm filler between the top of the quilt and the backing.

Batting

A wide choice of batting is available for the quilter. All battings available today are much improved over those our grandmothers and great-grandmothers used. They come in various weights and thicknesses, but the wise hand quilter will use a thin batting of whichever fiber content is desired.

Look for a high-quality batting that has a uniform thickness, is washable, and is easy to hand quilt. Hand quilting is an enjoyable experience if you have chosen the correct batting.

Other considerations to add to your checklist might include a batting that has a soft drape when quilted, a batting that is non-allergenic, and cost for the size batting you require. Like any consumer, you will need to read the product information on any batting you buy to make sure it meets your requirements.

Fiber Content of Batting

Cotton batting comes in a bleached white form or a natural, unbleached form. It can be bonded by surface starches or resins. Cotton battings can be blended with other fibers such as polyester, wool, and silk. They can be made more stable by needle-punch techniques or by the addition of scrims or other sub-straits. Cotton battings have many kinds of surface treatments—these treatments are applied or used in the creation of the batting to create the special features that will make it easier for the hand or machine quilter.

Make sure to buy the cotton batting to fit your hand quilting needs. Cotton blended with polyester or silk are the easiest to work by hand.

Silk batting is now a commonly available product. It usually comes as a blended or somewhat altered product to make it easier to use. The silk battings are ideal for thinner quilts needing the factor of extra warmth or for garments. They are easy to work by hand.

Wool batting has a natural color and is a highly resilient and warm filler for quilts. Most modern wool battings are pre-washed to reduce shrinkage. Wool is often added to other fibers for additional warmth and ease of hand needling. 100% wool batting is very easy to quilt by hand.

Synthetic, polyester battings are most commonly used for hand quilting. The thinner, needle-punched battings are easy to find and usually less expensive than the natural fiber battings. Select lower loft polyester battings for easy hand quilting. **Caution:** *Some heavier polyester batting sold in stores that sell upholstery fabrics do not have the same soft and pliable qualities as quilt battings.*

Tip: *Read the manufacturer's guidelines for the amount and quantity of hand quilting required for the batting you choose. Some require relatively little quilting, while some battings recommend quilting every quarter inch or so. Quilters who do not follow these guidelines are putting their quilts at risk for falling apart when being washed or wearing out prematurely.*

Tip: *Quilt shops and sewing stores that cater to quilters are your best source for quality battings.*

Preparing the Batting for Quilting

Remove the batting from the packaging the day before you intend to layer the quilt and unfold. The batting needs to relax, breathe and fluff. Most battings will have wrinkles or folds. To relax the wrinkles spray with water or a fabric softener commonly used when washing clothes.

Tip: *Remember—save the batting labels with the quilting and washing instructions.*

What to Quilt?

The designs and patterns for hand quilting are almost without number. Choosing what to hand quilt and where to put a suitable design is more of an art rather than a science. There are a few guidelines that I will mention here—but don't be too confined by tradition or convention. If you find you love hand quilting you will seek out just the right designs.

Look at quilts in museums, quilt shows and books to see what choices other quilters have made. There are few rules to guide you. There are many commercial quilt stencils and printed designs to use. Several quilts in this book have quilting designs that were prepared especially for that particular quilt. You'll recognize the hand quilting designs by the dash lines. A little later in this chapter there are instructions for making and using quilting stencils.

Caution: *Remember to keep in mind the amount of quilting required by the batting you choose when picking your quilting designs.*

Appliqué and Stenciled Quilts

Most appliqués and stencils are hand quilted very close to the edge of the design. If the design areas are large there probably should be some quilting within the appliquéd or stenciled design.

The area around the appliqué or stencil must also be quilted. There are several options including grids and shapes. (**Diagram 67**)

Diagram 67

Patchwork Quilts

Most patchwork is quilted 1/4" away from the seam edge or in-the-ditch of the seam line.

Overall hand quilting designs are also used and they include: all geometric shapes, diagonal lines, double diagonal lines, concentric squares, zigzag lines, stippling, basket weaves, feathers, garlands, and many other categories. (**Diagram 68**)

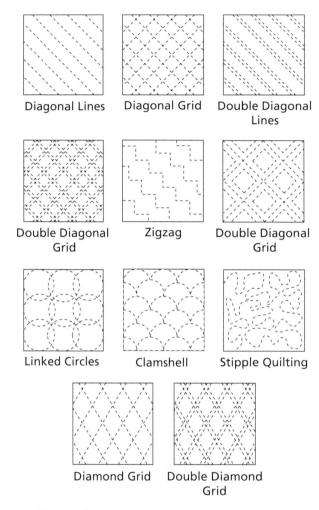

Diagram 68

Simple or elaborate designs can be quilted in larger open areas of patchwork. Under most circumstances the patterns chosen for hand quilting aren't either/or decisions. There are usually a wide variety of correct choices—feel free to experiment!

Quilting Stencils

Quilting stencils and designs sometimes look peculiar to beginning hand quilters. They usually come with little or no instructions for their use.

Stencils can be either "positive shapes" like the shape of a star or they can be a "negative hole" in a piece of paper or plastic. (**Diagram 69**)

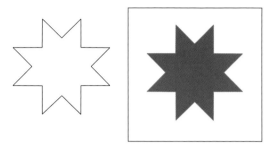

Diagram 69

Purchased stencils commonly come as designs pre-cut or punched in plastic or cardboard sheets. Stencils often have bridges connecting parts of the design. They are there to keep the stencil from falling apart. (**Diagram 70**)

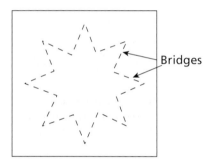

Diagram 70

Making a Stencil
Freezer Paper Technique

Copy the design you want onto the dull side of freezer paper—be accurate. If the design does not include bridges you will need to plan where these need to be. These stencils can be used as is, after cutting the design, or the freezer paper can be ironed onto lightweight file folders and then cut to create a sturdier stencil.

Tip: *Using your computer, make a photocopy of the quilting stencil. Scan the design into the computer and print onto freezer paper that has been hand trimmed to fit your printer.*

Contact Paper Technique

Contact paper has the advantage that it will stick to the fabric temporarily, and will reduce the need to otherwise mark the quilt. It can be placed, stitched around, and moved to the next location. Make a photocopy of the quilting design. Layer the copy over a trimmed piece of contact paper. Staple or pin the two together. Cut the design, leaving any bridges.

Thin Plastic

Lay the plastic over the design and trace with a marker. Cut out the design leaving the necessary bridges.

Layering the Quilt

This step is commonly called "making the quilt sandwich." This old saying will make sense when you first see or do the process.

1. Markings for hand quilting designs are placed before the quilt is layered. Center or position the stencils on the quilt top and mark with a removable pencil or marker. Mark all grid patterns or other necessary guidelines before layering the quilt.

2. Press the quilt back to remove any fold lines or wrinkles. Lay wrong side up on a table, floor or other flat surface. Over the backing, place the batting, smoothing it over the backing as you center it. Over the batting, place the quilt top smoothing, but not stretching, the fabric.

3. Next baste the quilt sandwich—the three layers—together with a needle and thread. Basting stitches are long. The basting lines generally are made from the center out toward the edges of the quilt. The lines of basting stitches should be no further apart than six inches.

Stitches Used for Quilting

Basting Stitch: This is a large hand stitch used to temporarily hold fabric or the layered quilt together. A fine hand stitch is then used and the basting is removed. Basting can be made without a hoop or frame. Begin with a single knotted thread. Take large, $1/2$" or longer, stitches.

The needle is pushed through the layers of the quilt horizontally. (**Diagram 71**)

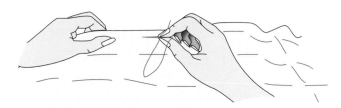

Diagram 71

Running Stitch: It is a finishing stitch and is made like a much smaller version of the basting stitch. The Running stitch can be completed without a hoop or frame. The stitch should be smaller than $1/4$" in length.

The needle is pushed through the layers of the quilt horizontally. (**Diagram 72**)

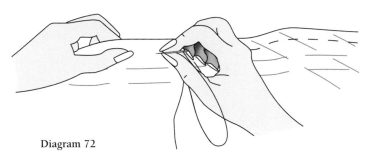

Diagram 72

Backstitch: It is a finishing stitch that can be used where a firmer stitch is wanted. It is used in conjunction with a Running stitch and a Dimple stitch. A discreet Backstitch is frequently used at the beginning and at the finish of a line of stitching to secure. (**Diagram 73**)

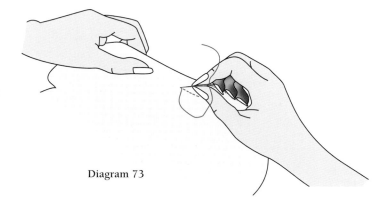

Diagram 73

Dimple Stitch: This stitch is frequently referred to as a stress-free quilting stitch because it puts less stress on the thumb, elbow and shoulders. It is a finishing stitch that is best and easier if made in a hoop or frame. A hoop allows both hands to be free for carrying out this stitch.

In the Dimple stitch, the needle is pushed through the quilt layers starting with the needle in a vertical position with the thimble alone on the needle and the thumb on the fabric in front of the needle. Each hand plays an important part in completing the Dimple Stitch. The fingers on the non-dominant hand (under the quilt) receive just the point of the needle. (**Diagram 74**)

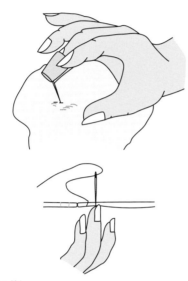

Diagram 74

The top, dominant hand simultaneously pushes the needle through the fabric and up towards the waiting thumb. (**Diagram 75**)

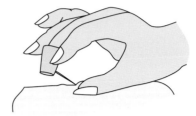

Diagram 75

Two or three more stitches might be taken in a "run" by alternating the vertical needle position and the push toward the thumb. (**Diagram 76**)

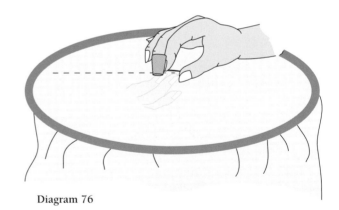

Diagram 76

Tip: *When learning the Dimple stitch, a beginner will usually take a one-stitch-at-a-time-approach. With confidence, and practice, more stitches will be taken in a single run.*

Using Hoops and Frames

Start quilting in the center of the project. Place the basted project over the lower half of the frame or hoop. Follow the manufacturer's instructions for placing the top of the hoop or frame.

Hoops

If your hoop is larger than the project, extend the size of the quilt by basting scrap fabric strips to the sides of the quilt. Baste through all three layers. (**Diagram 77**)

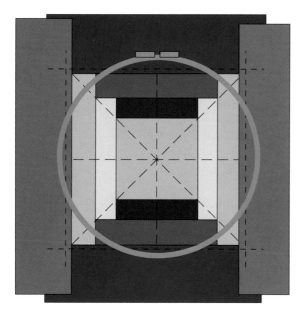

Diagram 77

Stretch the quilt firmly in the hoop. Check the top and bottom to see that there are no puckers or wrinkles. Then gently rub the heel of your hand over the smooth surface until the tension is relaxed and there is a slightly even sag in the quilt layers. My Grandma called this a "cat hammock."

Frames

Each style of quilting frame will have different instructions for attaching the different layers of the quilt.

When there is too great a difference in size between the quilt and the quilting frame, strips of scrap fabric can be basted to the sides of the quilt.

The Voice of Experience

When quilting elaborate quilt designs, stitch all straight lines on the frame; then take the quilt off the large frame and complete the more detailed work in a hoop on your lap.

Make threading easier by cutting the end of the thread at an angle.

Thread all your needles onto the spool of thread at one time...pull off and use as needed. (**Diagram 78**)

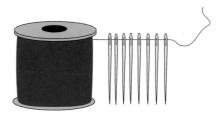

Diagram 78

Binding the Quilt

Straight-of-the-Grain Binding

A doubled, mitered binding is a good way to put the finishing touch on your quilt. Most quilts can use fabric strips cut on the straight of the grain. Take your time. It's worth the effort. Refer to individual quilt instructions for width of strips to cut for binding.

1. Place quilt on a large flat surface and trim excess backing and batting to the edge of the quilt top.

Tip: *Slip a large rotary mat under the quilt and use rotary tools to trim, measuring from the seam of the last border.*

2. Measure around the outside edges of the quilt. Join binding strips, on the diagonal, to that length. (see **Diagram 58**, page 163)

3. Fold the corner of the binding wrong sides together toward the edge at a 45-degree angle. Press firmly. Trim corner back to a generous 1/4". Fold binding over and press in half for the entire length. (**Diagram 79**)

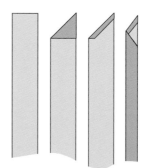

Diagram 79

171

4. Place folded binding along the edge of the front of the quilted top with raw edges even; begin sewing along one side with a generous $1/4$" seam allowance. When you approach to within $1/4$" of the corner, stop and pivot to a 45-degree angle and sew to the corner of the quilt. Lift presser foot but do not cut threads. (**Diagram 80**)

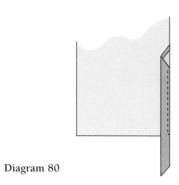

Diagram 80

Tip: *If you plan to bind the quilt totally by machine, start by sewing the binding on the wrong side of the quilt and bring the binding to the top side for a better machine finish. Machine stitch binding to quilt along folded edge.*

5. At the corner, fold the binding at a right (45-degree) angle, away from the quilt top. Fold back so that the binding is even with the next edge to be stitched. Lower the needle at the corner and continue sewing. This right angle corner tuck will create a full mitered corner when turned to the wrong side and hand stitched down. (**Diagram 81**) Repeat at remaining corners.

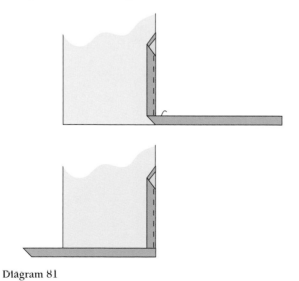

Diagram 81

6. To finish the end of the binding tuck the raw end into the folded end at the beginning of the binding and finish sewing. (**Diagram 82**)

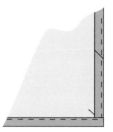

Diagram 82

7. Turn the binding to the opposite side of the quilt and stitch with a hidden stitch. Use a neutral thread. Close the mitered corner tuck with a few additional hand stitches.

Bias-Cut Mitered Binding

Under some circumstances, it is best to use bias strips for making the binding.

Use bias binding on curved corners or details so the bias strips will conform to the curves or when using small closely repetitive patterns such as checks or dots.

Bias binding was used on The Summertime quilt (page 122). This technique is used to control the fabric pattern.

1. Cut the required number of strips on the bias of the fabric according to individual pattern instructions. Join these strips on the bias. (**Diagram 83**)

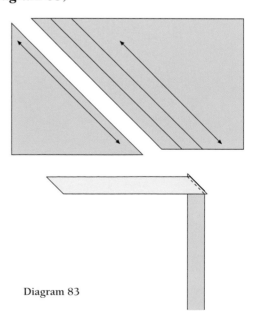

Diagram 83

Tip: *Don't stretch the bias strips as you press them. Use spray sizing or starch to help stabilize the fabric.*

2. Continue as for the Straight-of-the-Grain Binding, page 171 to 172.

How to Display Your Quilt

Small quilts can be hung by sewing a loop to the back of the quilt or by creating corner triangles that are stitched to the back of the quilt at the time of binding. Larger quilts require a simple sleeve.

Hanging Triangles

Depending on the size of your small quilt, cut two squares of fabric (3" to 6").

Fold each square in half diagonally with wrong sides together to form two triangles. (**Diagram 84**)

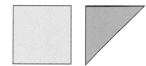

Diagram 84

Place triangles (folded squares) at the top of the backing of the small quilt before binding. (**Diagram 85**)

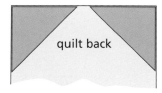

Diagram 85

Stitch the raw edges of the triangles into the binding. Insert a dowel or a chopstick into the triangle corners to hang. (**Diagram 86**)

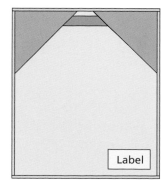

Diagram 86

Quilt Sleeve

The display sleeve can be stitched onto the quilt at the time of binding or can be applied to the back of the quilt at a later date.

Cut a length of backing fabric, or other fabric, the width of the quilt by 8" wide. Turn under and make a 1" hem at each end of the length. Fold the width in half wrong sides together and sew along the length of the sleeve to create a 3½" tube. Center seam in tube and press open. Sew this to the top of the back of the quilt. Display by inserting a pole through the sleeve. (**Diagram 87**)

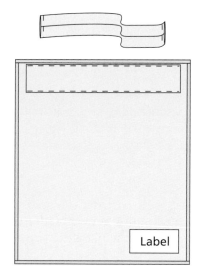

Diagram 87

Label

No quilt is truly finished until it has a label sewn to the back. People forget who has made a special quilt, even if it stays in the family. Don't let this happen to one of your quilts. The label can be plain or fancy, embroidered or written with permanent fabric markers, but it should contain the following information:

> ***Name of maker***
> ***Date***
> ***Location of maker***
> ***Occasion – if pertinent***

173

Quilt Care

Proper home care of quilts is important. If a quilt is newly constructed, one has more options than if a quilt is an antique or "vintage." Under any circumstances gentle quilt care is vital.

All quilts must be protected from soiling, direct sun, and normal household cleaning agents. Quilts should be stored in acid free paper and boxes or in clean cotton bags. Old pillowcases are good storage bags.

Stored quilts should be unrolled, turned and re-rolled two or three times a year to check for any changes in condition and to help prevent permanent fold marks.

Do not store quilts on raw wooden shelves or in wooden boxes without acid-free paper or cotton cloth between the quilt and the wood.

Antique quilts might need conservation and possible restoration by trained textile professionals. Quilts with missing stitches can be repaired by a skilled, non-professional needleworker. But anything more than a few stitches should be left to professionals.

Quilts that are used in normal domestic situations will need occasional, gentle cleansings.

Newer quilts may benefit from a gentle tumble in a large dryer, set to AIR ONLY, to remove dust, litter, or pet hair. Do not tumble vintage or antique quilts.

Most quilts can be used for some time without washing of any type. Even new quilts can be easily damaged by repeated washing and drying by machine. Quilts should never be washed with harsh detergents or bleach.

Blot-test each fabric before any spot cleaning or washing. Moisten fabric or stain with distilled water and cotton balls. Place a cotton ball under and over the moistened area. Blot by pushing the cotton balls together. Watch for staining by dye left in the fabric. **Caution:** *If a quilt is heavily soiled, any water, including the "Blot Test" is likely to leave a water-spot mark on the quilt fabric. If this happens on a new quilt, the entire quilt must be immersed and cleaned.*

Drying quilts on a clothesline is discouraged because the lack of proper weight distribution will damage the fabrics and the stitching threads.

If a quilt must be washed, do it in a clean, large tub with little agitation and a cleansing product recommended for quilts. Place a large folded bed sheet in the bottom of the tub. Do not remove excess water from the quilt by twisting the quilt. Force the water out of the fabric by kneading with the fists. Use the sheet to lift the damp quilt from the tub. **Caution:** *Make sure any product used to clean the tub is completely rinsed out of the tub before immersing a quilt in the tub for cleaning.*

Dry the washed and totally rinsed quilt on a large raised sling made from canvas or a strong sheet. The quilt should be made to dry quickly. A fan under and over the quilt is best. **Tip:** *A fabric sling can be fashioned between two lines on a clothesline or four or more posts driven into the ground.*

Rolling a damp quilt between dry towels to remove moisture is a good alternative to the sling method. The quilt is then spread on a clean sheet outside on the grass or inside on a clean sheet resting on clean carpet. Use fans to dry the quilt quickly. Do not allow anyone to walk on the quilt while it is drying and protect it from new soiling.

Do not dry clean quilts.

Metric Equivalents

inches	cm	inches	cm	inches	cm
1	2.54	11	27.94	21	53.34
2	5.08	12	30.48	22	55.88
3	7.62	13	33.02	23	58.42
4	10.16	14	35.56	24	60.96
5	12.70	15	38.10	30	76.20
6	15.24	16	40.64	36	91.44
7	17.78	17	43.18	42	106.68
8	20.32	18	45.72	48	121.92
9	22.86	19	48.26	54	137.16
10	25.40	20	50.80	60	152.40

Index